Birds of Lebanon
and the Jordan Area

Birds of Lebanon

and the Jordan Area

S. Vere Benson, M.B.O.U.
author of 'The Observer's Book of Birds'

With 94 species illustrated in colour and 258 in black and white, by the author

Foreword by Professor S. Dillon Ripley, Ph.D.

Published by
THE INTERNATIONAL COUNCIL FOR BIRD PRESERVATION
and distributed by
FREDERICK WARNE & CO LTD
LONDON & NEW YORK

First published by
The International Council for Bird Preservation
1970

In the publication of this book the financial assistance of the National Audubon Society U.S.A. and of the author is gratefully acknowledged

All profits from its sale will be given for the work of
The International Council for Bird Preservation

ISBN 0 7232 1289 9

Distributed by
Frederick Warne & Co Ltd, London & New York
Printed and bound in Great Britain by
W & J Mackay & Co Ltd, Chatham

CONTENTS

The author would like to express her appreciation to those responsible for the accurate and careful typesetting of a difficult manuscript and the skilful reproduction of the colour plates and line drawings in this book.

ACKNOWLEDGEMENTS

My warmest thanks to the following for answering my letters and enquiries while I was preparing this book: Mrs M. G. Eddy and Messrs †Carl Adolph Blume for 'Stop Press' records, †R. A. D. Cameron, including the valuable notes supplied, E. A. Chapman, including the loan of books, †*Lindon Cornwallis, I. J. Ferguson-Lees, including some notes in Appendix II, Anthony J. Gaston, Derek Goodwin, including kind and patient help and advice over many years, Poul Hald-Mortensen for records, Colin Harrison for advice, *Peter Hayman, including permission to sketch and reproduce his drawings and notes in Appendix I, P. A. D. Hollom, including much kind help and for reading this book in manuscript, S. Marchant, J. A. McGeoch, †Bent Pors Nielsen, including Aquila-Eagle notes in the journal of The Danish Ornithological Society, R. K. Norman, Richard Porter, *P. J. Stead, including the drawings and notes in Appendix I, and Kenneth Williamson; also to Dr Donald Broom, Dr James M. Harrison, including the loan of a skin of Dunn's Lark shot in Lebanon, Dr Ian Nisbet, *Dr John Raines, including permission to sketch and reproduce some of his silhouette photographs of flying eagles, and Dr Charles Vaurie; and much appreciation of the help given by Mr Charles Gouldson in reading proofs. I should also like to thank Mr Reginald Wagstaffe of the City of Liverpool Museum, and members of the staff, for kind help and the loan of skins for study and illustration, without which some of the more detailed illustrations could not have been made; and my grateful thanks for help received and for access to skins in the Royal Albert Memorial Museum of Exeter; also for much help over many years from members of the staff at the British Museum (Natural History), London. My thanks also to Professor R. E. Lewis and Dr J. Butros of the American University, Beirut; to the former for records and for kindly providing skins for study, also to the British Council, Beirut, for help and advice.

I am much obliged to Mr Karnig Chahinian of Beirut, to whom many thanks for the loan of his little car in 1964.

Above all, my most grateful thanks and indebtedness to *Dr W. R. P. Bourne for reading this book in manuscript and for innumerable helpful suggestions and criticisms, as well as information and Cyprus records, and for his untiring patience over details, even when more than fully occupied with his own responsibilities. Without his help and encouragement, the work would have been seriously hindered and incomplete.

S.V.B.

* Contributors to Appendix I.

† See Introduction, pages xv, xvi.

COLOUR PLATES

THE LEBANON

N
W
E
S
El Arida
Machta Hassan
Chadra
Amirie
El Biri
Andakat
Qoubayat
N. Ostouene
Halba
Ain Yaaqoub
Rahbe
Habchite
Fnaidek
Nahr abou Moussa
El Minie
Nahr el Bared
Nakl Js.
TRIPOLI
Kafra Hadou
Sir
Bkaa Safrine
Zghorta
Miziara
Enfé
Chekka
Bechmezzin
Amioun
Kosba
Ehden
KORNET es SAOUDA 3083 m
The CEDARS
Bcharre
Hadeth
Hasroun
Batroun
Nahr el Jaouz
LEBANON RANGE
Hermel
Nahr el Assi
Ras Baalbek
Laboué
Ainata
B E K A A
Ain Bayada
Lakloukh
Aqoura
Jabal el Mnaitri 2702
El Yammouné
Deir el Ahmar
Maqne
Chlifa
BIBLOS (JBAIL)
Nahr Ibrahim
Yahchouch
Afqa
Faraya
Ghazir
Jounie
Harissa
el Kelb
BAALBEK
ANTI LEBANON

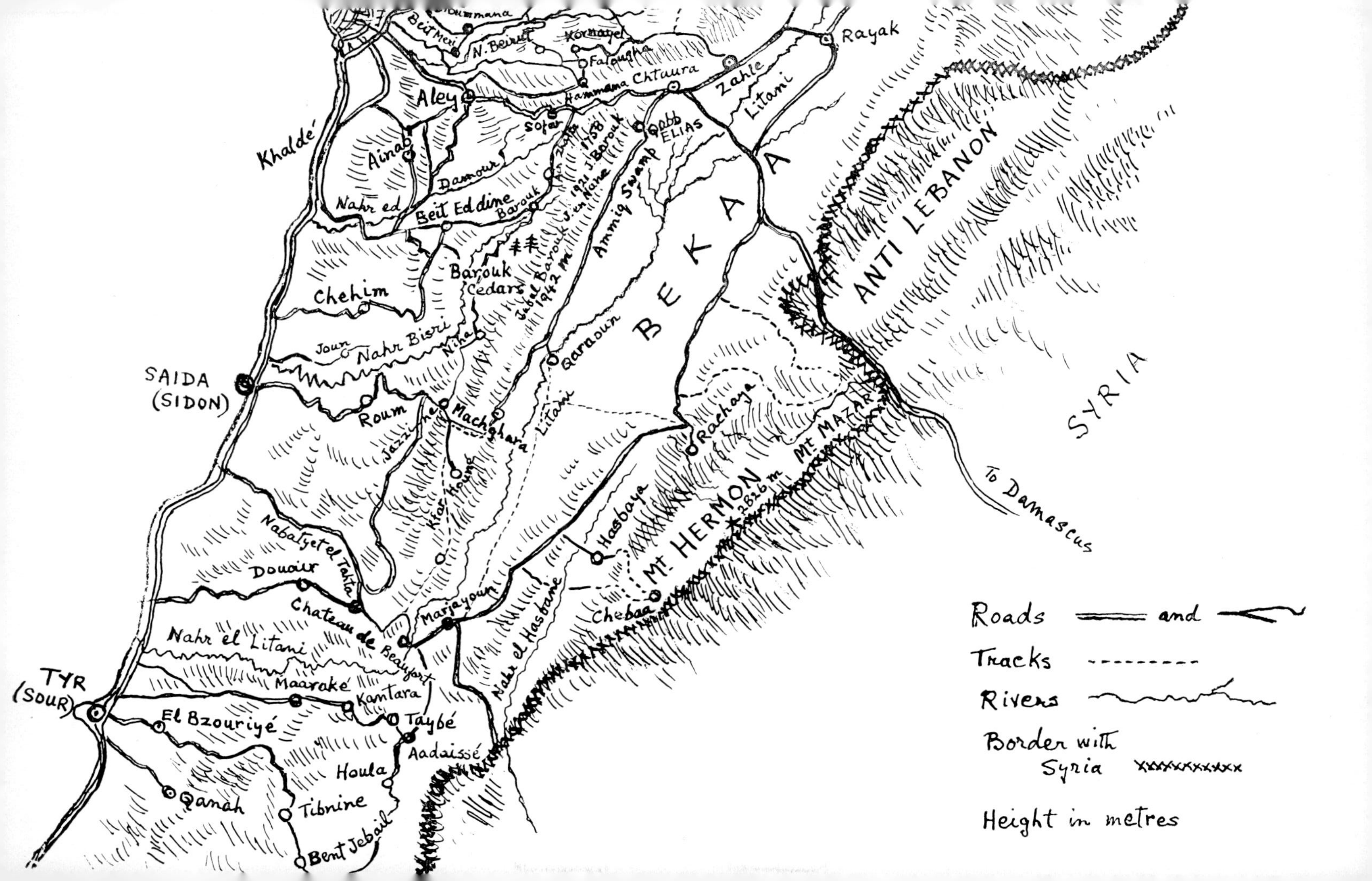

Rayak
Zahle
Litani
Ch'taura
Hammana
Falougha
Kornayel
N. Beirut
Beit Meri
Aley
Sofar
Khaldé
Ainab
Damour
Nahr ed
Beit Eddine
Barouk
Qobb ELIAS
Ammiq Swamp
Barouk Cedars
Jebel Barouk
1942 m
B E K A A
ANTI LEBANON
SYRIA
Chehim
Joun
Nahr Bisri
Niha
SAIDA (SIDON)
Roum
Machghara
Jezzine
Qaraoun
Litani
Kfar Houne
Rachaya
Mt MAZAR
Mt HERMON
2826 m
To Damascus
Nabatyet el Takta
Douair
Hasbaya
Chebaa
Marjayoun
Chateau de Beaufort
Nahr el Litani
Nahr el Hasbane
TYR (SOUR)
Maaraké
Kantara
Taybé
El Bzouriyé
Aadaissé
Houla
Qanah
Tibnine
Bent Jebail
Roads and
Tracks
Rivers
Border with Syria
Height in metres

TO

FAY AND ANTHONY

Remembering old times and their
unstinted help and hospitality

FOREWORD

Slowly, like adding stone by stone on to a cairn at the top of the pass, human travellers in this world of ours begin to understand the implications of their existence and their surroundings. In this process more and more of us must continue to find hope that future generations, the young and very young, and those still unborn, will gradually achieve a level of such education and understanding that they will be able to live in peace with their surroundings. Few places in the world exhibit more dramatically the potential for destruction by man than the Middle Eastern and Near Eastern countries of the eastern Mediterranean east to Bengal. In classic times the greatest achievements of the world in the development of agriculture through irrigation were achieved here. However, a parallel effort first unnoticed then developing, gradually diminished the effectiveness of this breakthrough in agricultural technology. This effort consisted first of the domestication of sheep and goats which in succeeding millennia became the scourge of these countries, and also the ceaseless rivalries and warfare of the rulers, tribes and ethnic groups themselves which has kept so much of the area from achieving eventual stability and peace. Agriculture and peace must go hand-in-hand and with them the chances for education and self-fulfilment of the yearning human population. Until such a day comes, it remains for us to hope that the continued slow progress in these directions will not be too late for the other warm-blooded creatures and the plants that share this part of the planet with us.

A book on birds in a country like the Lebanon epitomizes all the things we wish and hope for. If only more education were available for the young, if only more stability was available for those who are in the seats of government, and if only more progressive and thoughtful methods of agriculture could once again become dominant, then there is a chance that not only the birds of Lebanon would be happy but the people also. The fate of the birds of Lebanon exercises a solemn and prophetic warning for the continuance of the nation itself. It is not too dramatic or too theatrical to say that when birds themselves finally become extinct throughout this country, the last warning gong may have sounded. Curiously enough, people often pay heed to serious events of this sort almost at the very last moment, hovering on the brink, as it were. It would appear that present studies on the indiscriminate use of pesticides may alone have a significant effect on public opinion, enough to pull human-kind back from the brink of another potential disaster. If the present rate of absorption of chemicals in the bodies of plants and animals is continued, it seems likely that the effect will be serious enough to make even the most heedless person pay attention and literally demand a change in public understanding and a turn towards a more universal public education.

Miss Vere Benson has done a signal service to all of those of us concerned with the economy and the over-all health and welfare of the countries of the eastern Mediterranean by the publication of this handbook on the birds of Lebanon. Here in microcosm can be seen many of the evidences of the conditions of which we are all aware and of which many of us speak and think unceasingly. Here then is a chance to educate the very young, and to attempt to create a setting, out of which informed public opinion can arise. Thus a hobby can be turned to a foundation stone for future progress, one stone piled upon another may help create a sense of understanding and fulfilment in years to come.

S. DILLON RIPLEY

Smithsonian Institution
Washington, D.C.

President, International Council
for Bird Preservation

INTRODUCTION

Lebanon has a very interesting bird population and because of its geographical position has a passage migration much more spectacular than most countries can boast, including many surprising visitors.

The purpose of this book is, firstly, to give a field guide, as complete as possible, for bird-watchers living in or visiting Lebanon or neighbouring countries. With this aim in view, a Check List is provided of all birds so far recorded within the borders of Lebanon. This list is constantly being added to as bird-watching in the country progresses. For Jordan a further list is given in Appendix 2. These are birds not yet recorded in Lebanon, though many of the migrant ones may occur.

It is realized that large numbers of the birds passing through the area are common to Europe, and that these are already more fully described and illustrated in other books, but it is hoped that their inclusion here will be helpful not only to those who do not already possess these other books, but to all who want a balanced survey of the birds of Lebanon in all seasons.

Most of the species are fully described, but there is an additional list of birds which have seldom been recorded here and which really belong to other areas. These are of less significance in describing the ornithology of Lebanon, and only a brief plumage description and summary of their general range and their status in Lebanon is given.

The two colour plates, numbers 5 and 7, were added when the Arabic edition was planned, and are intended specially for the members of the Lebanese League for Bird Preservation and for students and school children in Lebanon who may not see a European field guide to birds. If they are not in keeping with the other plates it is because they had to show so many small birds, some of them visiting Lebanon infrequently, half of them from Europe.

The second purpose is to provide adequate detail for the identification of the birds of the Levant found in Lebanon, and it will be noticed that more space has been given to these than to the other species. Some of these are unknown or unfamiliar in Europe, and new ground has been covered here. Some of the birds included lack detailed illustrations and descriptions in other books, and in fact very little has been known or written about them. Persistent efforts have been made to study all available skins of these and to illustrate them in detail and with the spread wing where this is of diagnostic importance. The third purpose—see page xviii.

THE ORDER AND THE RECORDS

The order and classification of species and subspecies in this book follow Charles Vaurie in *The Birds of the Palearctic Fauna*, as also the order, names and division of families. Subfamilies are considered unnecessary in a book of this type.

In one or two cases where there is a difference of opinion as to the validity of a species or as to whether a certain subspecies should be considered a species, the matter has been mentioned. The records, though added to in recent years, are based on H. Kumerloeve's *Notes on the Birds of the Lebanese Republic*, an invaluable collection of all ancient and modern records with the status of each species.

It is probable that bird-watchers may at first be confused by the plumage differences between various races of larks and other small Passerine birds in the Levant. They often vary in colour very greatly. For example, one of the races of *Calandrella rufescens*, the Lesser Short-toed Lark, in the Middle East is described by Vaurie as pale reddish sandy, another as pale sandy grey. To the bird-watcher familiar with the race in southern Spain, which is darker, greyer and more heavily spotted on the breast, the southern Levant birds may look confusingly like all the other small sandy-coloured larks of deserts and hills. For this reason, and in spite of the fact that descriptions of races and subspecies, or even mention of them, may be frowned upon in a book of this nature, I have felt it necessary to refer to and describe several of them.

THE GREAT RAPTOR MIGRATION

The great autumn passage of eagles and other birds of prey which passes along the western slopes of Lebanon, not far from the coast, has to be seen to be believed. This wonderful sight is also mentioned under the heading of each of these species. When I first saw it after sunrise below Aley, I could scarcely believe the evidence of my eyes as about 400 eagles passed over in forty-five minutes.

From notes taken in 1963 it seems that the main passage started on the 16th September with a thin stream of Honey Buzzards which I recorded flying south, fairly low, between Beirut and the western slopes of the Lebanon range. On the 18th and 22nd the passage was increasing, reaching its peak on the 23rd when at least 500 passed during only half an hour's watching. Peak hours were the first two after the sun had risen over the mountain range to the east. By the 23rd the full passage of eagles was under way, chiefly consisting of Spotted and hundreds of Lesser Spotted Eagles and two or three separate groups of Griffon Vultures. Besides these, I was able to identify a few Egyptian Vultures, Bonelli's and Booted Eagles, two immature Golden Eagles and one immature White-tailed Eagle, plus a multitude too far off for identification. There were also a large number of small hawks, a few Goshawks and some Harriers, chiefly Marsh Harriers. Buzzards were not in great numbers by this date.

R. A. D. Cameron and L. Cornwallis, in notes prepared for publication, describe a passage of eagles and other birds of prey, also near the Lebanon coast-line, during the week following my records. The only other published records which I have come across bearing at all on the autumn migration of these species in or near Lebanon are from North Syria by G. A. Pyman.

The notes made by Cameron and Cornwallis in September 1963 cover five days from 25th to 29th, before the end of which time the highest peak in numbers had passed. The species identified during these days were almost the same as those which I recorded during the previous week. During the five days a total was seen of 124 Egyptian Vultures, 13 Griffon Vultures, 9 Golden Eagles, 1,232 Spotted and Lesser Spotted Eagles with probably a few Steppe Eagles, 3 Bonelli's, 27 Booted and 287 unspecified Eagles. There were also 497 Common Buzzards with a few Long-legged and Rough-legged and 364 unspecified Buzzards, 1,552 Sparrow Hawks and Levant Sparrow Hawks, 16 Goshawks, a few Kites, Honey Buzzards, Harriers, Kestrels and Peregrines, and 52 Short-toed Eagles besides another 2,600 unspecified birds of prey, making a grand total of 6,865. Most of the unspecified birds passed too far away to be identified with any accuracy. The watching was from a crag just below Harissa.

My own experience of the late September passage was repeated in 1964, when at the same place as in 1963, below Aley, a friend and I watched about 400 mixed eagles pass over in forty-five minutes in the early morning. The weather was hot and dry and the pressure high on the western side of the range, and the eagles were too high for us to make out much detail. However, the majority appeared to be Lesser Spotted with an uncertain number of Spotted and Steppe Eagles. With difficulty we also managed to make out four other species.

Suddenly out of the sky, about 80 to 100 little hawks appeared like a cloud of mosquitoes. They looked very small in comparison with the eagles and were almost certainly Levant Sparrow Hawks which are known to flock like this. Almost as suddenly as they had appeared, they seemed to find an up-current of air and to go up like a swirl of dust to an altitude at which they disappeared. References to this phenomenon are given by other writers and may be found in *Ibis* where Colonel Meinertzhagen describes the use of thermals by migrating Storks, Gulls and raptors. These thermals appear to be most common over hot plains, valleys or lakes. On other occasions I saw the eagles making use of them over the Lebanon range, and on this occasion it was evident that the hawks were spiralling upward in a thermal which carried them very high before they glided on again. I picked up the migration stream again some miles further south during an evening watch when about fifty large *Aquila* Eagles were passing over.

'Stop Press' news, from Mr Bent Pors Nielsen and from other experienced Danish ornithologists, of the raptor migration in the autumns of 1968 and 1969, mentions the passage of 24 species numbering about 16,000 birds. These passed through during four days watching in late September 1968 and nine days in September-October 1969. The records include 20 immature Steppe Eagles in 1969 (the first time this species has been counted while passing through Lebanon); also, during the two autumn counts, a total of over 2,500 Levant Sparrows Hawks, nearly 5,500 Honey Buzzards and well over 6,000 Lesser Spotted Eagles were recorded at Harissa.

HABITATS

The Lebanon comprises 10,000 square kilometres, an area only about 31 miles wide by 156 miles long, in the centre of the eastern end of the Mediterranean shore. It has a great deal of sunshine and very seldom gets any rain between May and October. Autumn migrants may suffer from the heat and drought. The high mountains are covered with snow in winter and early spring and the mountain birds are then mostly driven to lower altitudes.

The heights of the Lebanon range dominate the landscape, especially from the centre of the narrow coastal strip northward. There are lower hills in the north-west and south.

The mountains are full of Lesser Whitethroats and Sardinian Warblers flitting about secretively in the rather dry, generally prickly scrub. In the more luxuriant scrub and taller bushes, and in valleys with trees or hills with groups of umbrella-shaped pines, Blackcaps, Great Tits, Greenfinches and Chaffinches are very common, and Orphean Warblers are fairly plentiful. The Bulbuls are chiefly to be found in suburban gardens and thickets, in olive groves and the moister valleys with trees by rivers, and in the orange and banana plantations at no great altitude; and the Graceful Warblers along the coast in scrub, herbage and rubble.

From Beirut the nearest good river valleys are those of the Beirut river, Nahr Beyrouth, joined by the Nahr el Météne; also that of the Nahr el Kelb 15 kilometres north along the main coastal road. But all river valleys are profitable for bird watching.

The famous old Cedars, dating back to the Old Testament, which have been reduced to a group of only 400 trees, some being 1,500 years old, or more, stand at an altitude of over 6,000 feet, about 105 kilometres from Beirut, and can be reached by following the main coastal road northward to Tripoli and turning off to the right to the mountains at Chekka, or by another turning just before reaching Tripoli, and passing through Amioun, Kousba, Hadeth, Hasroun and Bcharré, up winding roads and hair-pin bends near which the Persian Robin has been seen, past the habitats of Cretzschmar's Buntings, Shrikes of four different species, Wood and Crested Larks, and a number of warblers, wheatears and finches. The last part of the drive from Bcharré up narrow, steep hair-pin bends to the Cedars is spectacular, as the road overlooks the Kadisha gorge, habitat of hundreds of Rock Sparrows, with Blue Rock Thrushes perched on rocks overlooking the road and Rock Nuthatches frequenting the precipitous cliffs. The Cedars themselves stand in a small plateau flanked by a semi-circle of the higher summits, the highest of which, the Kornet es Suada, reaches just above 10,000 feet. These heights are the habitat of the Raven and Kestrel, and sometimes the Alpine Chough and smaller uncommon birds, and the steep, bare slopes leading up to them are populated with Chukar partridges, Rock Buntings, Black Redstarts (Asian form, half red), Wheatears of several kinds, including Isabelline, Horned Larks, and sometimes by many flocks of Crimson-winged Finches gathering for their local autumn movements. Tristram's Serins are not uncommon and Tawny Pipits are everywhere in ones and twos.

In times of migration the Cedars themselves may be full of many kinds of birds, but at other times they have a population of Chaffinches and Tits, with a few Hooded Crows, Bee-eaters, Mistle Thrushes, Spotted Flycatchers, Greenfinches and other familiar birds.

A very rough, rocky road, often impassable, leads in a series of zigzags over the high mountain ridge to Ainata several thousand feet below on the far side. But the best way to reach this place is to go east from Beirut on the main Damascus road, over the mountains by the pass of Dahr el Baidan, 5000 feet up, and down the other side to the plain of Bekaa (part of the Great Rift Valley), itself over 3,000 feet above sea level, where a straight road leads to Baalbek. From Baalbek, after crossing the Bekaa, a rocky, rough road or track leads to Ainata, about 5,500 feet up through Deir el Ahmar. These hills are well populated with warblers, including Upcher's Warbler, above and below Ainata, and with Chukars, Hooded Crows, Jays, Doves, Cuckoos, and some Great Spotted Cuckoos; also with Nightjars, Nightingales, Wheatears of several species, including an occasional one or two Finsch's Wheatears in or near ravines or perched on a rock, but these are possibly more frequent on the western side of the mountains. Other birds of this area are Larks of several species, Great and Sombre Tits (Coal Tits occur chiefly in the cedars and pines), Tawny Pipits and a few Long-billed Pipits, several species of Shrikes and a variety of finches including a few small parties of Crimson-winged Finches and many Linnets, Buntings and Rock Sparrows, with a few Long-legged Buzzards and Kestrels. Hobbies are more frequent on the lower western hills with pines, as are also Kestrels.

A so-called village of two or three small buildings, often called Mchaityé or M'chatie, but not signposted as such, between Deir el Ahmar and Ainata, seems to be the best area for Sombre Tits, and is also good for Tristram's Serins.

Other places with special habitats are the Ammiq Swamp, southern cedars area, Litani river (Leontes) surroundings, also the Hermon and Anti-Lebanon ranges, especially the neighbourhood of Rachaya, where the Persian Robin once bred. Extreme north and south Lebanon should also be visited, as well as the hills and valleys of the western slopes of the Lebanon range which are easily accessible by road. The best bushy woodland of central Lebanon is here, especially in the areas inland from Beirut. In the north, the Wadi Chadra, leading to the northern border with Syria, is wooded along the river side.

THE MAP

The map provided here is unavoidably lacking in detail and limited in accuracy. A more detailed map is almost a necessity, but difficulties may occur over the names of places which are so variably spelt on different maps and in different books that it is often difficult to recognize the names of the villages.

CONSERVATION

The third, and most urgent, purpose of this book is to encourage conservation. It is greatly hoped that the realization of the precarious position of Lebanon's breeding birds through persistent shooting, and the awful slaughter of her migrant ones, together with an appreciation of the unique value of her geographical position on the great migration routes between three continents, will encourage the Government and the people of this beautiful country to preserve their bird population and restrict the unceasing destruction of the birds.

Most of the species which come to breed are destroyed in the midst of their nesting preparations, and there are a number of resident or formerly resident species which are now either extinct or nearly so, or possibly clinging to existence in the less accessible part of the mountains.

Amongst the breeding birds which are in danger of extinction here (to mention only a few) are the resident and summering owls and birds of prey, while the smaller birds, the larks and buntings, wheatears and nightingales are so persecuted by shooters that they have a much lower breeding success than they should have; and the Bee-eaters' efforts to breed seem to have been completely unsuccessful of late. These colourful birds and the equally beautiful Rollers are slaughtered unremittingly. The shy and rare Persian Robin is also unlikely to succeed even if it still attempts to stay and breed, and the three kinds of Kingfishers are in little better case.

As for the Waders and water birds, with so little suitable habitat in which to shelter, they are picked off almost at once, and from the scantiness of records it would appear that they are usually carried off before any interested recorder has had time to see them. The Kentish and Little Ringed Plovers, for instance, stand little chance of survival for breeding.

The only habitats for large and small water birds are the little swamps and reed-beds now being drained near Ammiq, and the edges of some of the rivers. But the Ammiq Swamp is heavily shot over and all the larger birds are killed. It is doubtful if very many of the smaller ones survive throughout the breeding season either.

If a real determination to preserve this heritage of beauty and interest could prevail, and the Ammiq Swamp area and considerable areas in the mountains, where trees and bushes give shelter, could be set aside as National Park Reserves where no shooting is allowed at any time of year, this would, indeed, be an asset to Lebanon.

The great hope is that more of the influential people of this country, with authority to do something lasting in the present critical situation, will realize that the birds of Lebanon are something to be proud of, and will reserve areas for breeding birds, and for rest and food for migrants on passage, jealously guarded for this purpose by the will of the people and Government.

This concept might also be introduced in schools and in young people's movements such as Boy Scouts.

Another urgent need is for the strictest control of toxic chemicals which destroy birds, or which have far-reaching repercussions on them. One resident in the country recently wrote to me saying 'The tremendous use of insecticide is terrible and I don't know what can be done about it.' The way it is used in Lebanon is not only destructive to birds, insects and some mammals, but already seems to be a menace to the people, especially those who appear to be spraying in the fields with little or no protection for themselves.

The diminution of trees and shrubs and the general erosion of the country is another factor which makes it essential to have Reserves set aside for the preservation of all forms of life, including woods and bushes.

Birds which were breeding freely before the great erosions and the advent of cars and guns, such as Booted, Imperial and Golden Eagles, Levant Sparrow Hawk, Barn, Tawny, Long-eared and Eagle-Owls, now lack the old forests and other suitable cover, and have either been driven out, or have been much reduced, as in the case of Scops and Little Owls.

Doubt about the breeding of many species is disappointing. Resident and summering birds behave here rather differently from those in neighbouring countries. In Jordan birds building nests or feeding young are seen in plenty, but here they have become secretive and skulking and nests are difficult to locate. Some species have had to confine themselves to nesting sites as far as possible from human reach.

THE INTERNATIONAL COUNCIL FOR BIRD PRESERVATION, AND THE LEBANESE LEAGUE FOR BIRD PRESERVATION

In view of the fact that the I.C.B.P. are publishing this book, I must express my appreciation of the great help and encouragement received from Miss Phyllis Barclay-Smith, Secretary-General of the I.C.B.P., and my admiration of the vigorous and inspiring way in which she has carried forward the idea of this publication in support of an urgent bid to save the birds of Lebanon.

The L.L.B.P. was founded in January 1967 and officially authorized by a Decree of the Lebanese Government, thanks to the efforts of its founder-President, Mr Hussein Abbas Kaidbey. This League needs much wider support and encouragement.

It is hoped that the sale of this book will strengthen further progress, especially if the Arabic edition to be published soon for the use of the Lebanese League and for all students in Lebanon, meets with success and is used in Lebanese schools. The birds described are also found in all the neighbouring countries, especially in Syria and Jordan, and the species in Jordan which do not penetrate as far north as Lebanon are described in Appendix II.

I am very grateful to Professor Dillon Ripley, President of I.C.B.P. for his Foreword, and for his support of this effort to preserve the birds of Lebanon for posterity.

S. VERE BENSON
(Mrs Wynne Taylor)

Bude, Cornwall. 1970.

TOPOGRAPHY OF A BIRD

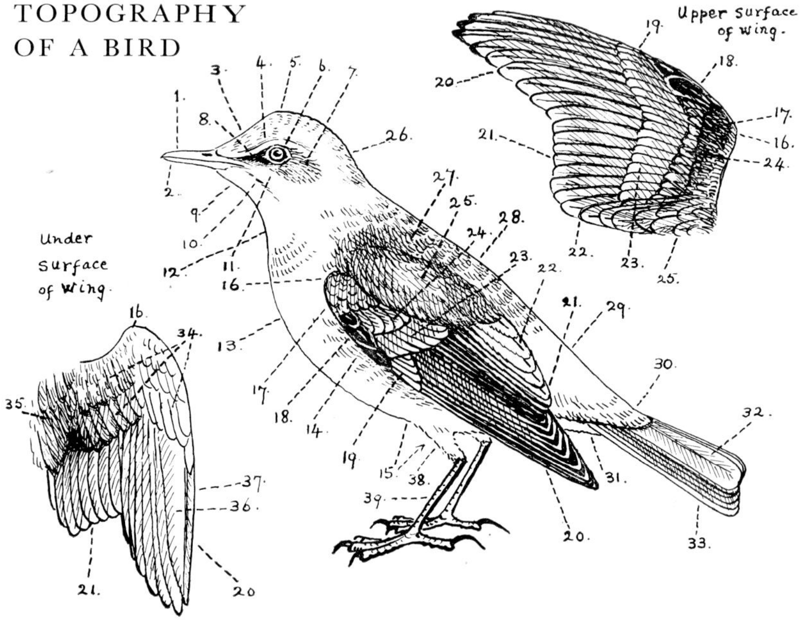

1. Upper mandible } Bill
2. Lower mandible } Bill
3. Forehead
4. Superciliary stripe
5. Crown
6. Eye-ring
7. Ear-coverts
8. Lores
9. Chin
10. Moustachial stripe
11. Cheek
12. Throat
13. Breast
14. Flank
15. Belly (Abdomen)
16. Bend of wing (carpal joint)
17. Lesser wing-coverts
18. Winglet (Alula)
19. Primary-coverts
20. Primaries
21. Secondaries
22. Inner secondaries
23. Greater wing-coverts
24. Median wing-coverts
25. Scapulars
26. Nape
27. Mantle
28. Back
29. Rump
30. Upper tail-coverts
31. Under tail-coverts
32. Tail-feathers
33. Outer tail-feathers
34. Under wing-coverts
35. Axillaries
36. Inner web of feather
37. Outer web of feather
38. Thigh
39. Leg (Tarsus)

Speculum: Wing-bar of Duck (see page 193).

AUTHOR'S NOTE

Topography (see page xxi):

The greater, median and lesser wing-coverts are included in the term 'upper wing-coverts' in this book. Sometimes in descriptions the term 'under wing-coverts' is shortened to 'under-wing', and where the meaning is made clearer by the use of words joined by extra hyphens (not in use on page xxi) these have been used in certain descriptions.

CHECK-LIST

Some of the birds listed below are both migrants and breeding species, some are common migrants of which a few stay for the winter. There are also species with a resident race here and many other migrant races passing through to and from Europe and northern Asia, so these must be shown as residents and migrants. The abbreviations printed against the name of each bird give an idea of the status of each species as far as it is known, and the order in which the abbreviations are given indicates the order of importance of each category, as far as is possible. For example, the Levant Sparrow Hawk, by noting the order of the abbreviations, should be understood to be an abundant passage migrant here, also occurring in winter, and possibly breeding or it used to breed here; whereas the Lesser Whitethroat is shown to be an abundant summer visitor found all over the Lebanon range and breeding commonly. It is also a migrant in spring and autumn here.

PM = Passage Migrant, WV = Winter Visitor, SV = Summer Visitor, R = Resident, B = Breeds, Has B = has bred, V = Vagrant, A = Abundant, C = Common, S = Scarce, O = Occasional. Square brackets = unproved records.

This list of birds may be marked off and dated as a record of the species you have seen.

PM, WV, B?	LITTLE GREBE
WV, V	BLACK-NECKED GREBE
V	RED-NECKED GREBE
WV	GREAT CRESTED GREBE
PM	CORY'S SHEARWATER
PM	MANX SHEARWATER
PM	WHITE PELICAN
PM	DALMATIAN PELICAN
V	PINK-BACKED PELICAN
WV	GANNET
V	CORMORANT
WV, V	PYGMY CORMORANT
WV, S	BITTERN
PM, B?	LITTLE BITTERN
PM, S	NIGHT HERON
PM	SQUACCO HERON
V	CATTLE EGRET
PM, C	LITTLE EGRET

PM, S	GREAT WHITE EGRET
PM	GREY HERON
PM	PURPLE HERON
PM, O, V	SPOONBILL
V	GLOSSY IBIS
PM, C	WHITE STORK
PM, O, V	BLACK STORK
V	GREATER FLAMINGO
WV, S	WHITE-FRONTED GOOSE
V	[BEAN GOOSE]
V	RUDDY SHELDUCK
WV, S, V	SHELDUCK
WV, PM	MALLARD
PM, WV	TEAL
PM, WV, S	WIGEON
PM, WV	PINTAIL
PM, O	GARGANEY
PM, WV, S	SHOVELER
WV, S	POCHARD
PM, WV, O	FERRUGINOUS DUCK
V	VELVET SCOTER
V	GOLDENEYE
PM	OSPREY
A, PM	HONEY BUZZARD
V	BLACK-WINGED KITE
V	KITE
PM, WV, C	BLACK KITE
V	WHITE-TAILED EAGLE
PM, WV	GOSHAWK
A, PM, WV, B?	LEVANT SPARROW HAWK
PM, WV, B?	SPARROW HAWK
R, B, PM	LONG-LEGGED BUZZARD
A, PM, C, WV	BUZZARD
V	ROUGH-LEGGED BUZZARD
PM, B?	BOOTED EAGLE
PM, B	BONELLI'S EAGLE
PM, WV	STEPPE EAGLE
PM, WV	SPOTTED EAGLE
A, PM	LESSER SPOTTED EAGLE
PM, B?	IMPERIAL EAGLE
PM, B?	GOLDEN EAGLE
PM, C, B, R?	EGYPTIAN VULTURE
PM, B, R?	GRIFFON VULTURE

V	BLACK VULTURE
PM, SV, B	SHORT-TOED EAGLE
PM	PALLID HARRIER
PM	MONTAGU'S HARRIER
PM, WV	HEN HARRIER
PM, WV, SV, B?	MARSH HARRIER
PM, WV?	SAKER
PM, WV?, B?	LANNER
PM, B?	PEREGRINE
PM	ELEONORA'S FALCON
PM, SV, B, C	HOBBY
PM, WV, S?	MERLIN
PM	RED-FOOTED FALCON
PM, SV, B	LESSER KESTREL
R, B, C	KESTREL
R, B, C	CHUKAR PARTRIDGE
A, PM, SV, B?	QUAIL
PM, O	CRANE
PM, O	DEMOISELLE CRANE
V	GREAT BUSTARD
V	LITTLE BUSTARD
V	HOUBARA
PM, WV, B?	WATER RAIL
PM	SPOTTED CRAKE
PM	[LITTLE CRAKE]
PM?	[BAILLON'S CRAKE]
PM	CORNCRAKE
R, B, PM, WV	MOORHEN
PM, WV, B?	COOT
V?	[PURPLE GALLINULE]
V	OYSTERCATCHER
PM	RINGED PLOVER
PM	LITTLE RINGED PLOVER
PM	KENTISH PLOVER
PM	GREATER SAND PLOVER
V	CASPIAN PLOVER
PM, WV, S	DOTTEREL
PM, S	GREY PLOVER
V	SOCIABLE PLOVER
PM, WV	LAPWING
PM, S	SPUR-WINGED PLOVER
PM, S?	LITTLE STINT
PM, O	TEMMINCK'S STINT

PM, WV?	DUNLIN
PM, O	[CURLEW SANDPIPER]
V	KNOT
PM, O	SANDERLING
PM, O?	RUFF
PM, O	BROAD-BILLED SANDPIPER
PM, O	REDSHANK
PM, O	GREENSHANK
PM	GREEN SANDPIPER
PM, O	WOOD SANDPIPER
PM, C, WV	COMMON SANDPIPER
PM, O	WHIMBREL
PM, WV	WOODCOCK
PM, WV	COMMON SNIPE
PM	GREAT SNIPE
WV, PM, S?	JACK SNIPE
PM, S	BLACK-WINGED STILT
PM, S	AVOCET
PM, B?, S?	STONE CURLEW
O, B?	CREAM-COLOURED COURSER
PM	PRATINCOLE
PM	BLACK-WINGED PRATINCOLE
V	HEMPRICH'S GULL
V	GREAT BLACK-HEADED GULL
PM, WV	MEDITERRANEAN BLACK-HEADED GULL
WV	LITTLE GULL
WV, C, PM	BLACK-HEADED GULL
PM, WV, O	SLENDER-BILLED GULL
PM, C, WV, SV	LESSER BLACK-BACKED GULL
PM, C, WV, SV, B	HERRING GULL
O. PM?, WV?	GREAT BLACK-BACKED GULL
WV, S	COMMON GULL
V, Has B	AUDOUIN'S GULL
PM	WHITE-WINGED BLACK TERN
V	GULL-BILLED TERN
V, Has B	LESSER CRESTED TERN
V	SANDWICH TERN
PM, Has B	COMMON TERN
PM, Has B	LITTLE TERN
WV, O	WOOD PIGEON
R, B	ROCK DOVE
PM, C, SV, B	TURTLE DOVE

R, B, C	PALM DOVE
PM, C, SV, B	CUCKOO
PM, SV, B	GREAT SPOTTED CUCKOO
V, B?	EAGLE OWL
V	BROWN FISH-OWL
WV, O	LONG-EARED OWL
WV	SHORT-EARED OWL
R, B, PM	SCOPS OWL
R, B, C	LITTLE OWL
S, B?	TAWNY OWL
S, B?	BARN OWL
PM, C, SV, B	NIGHTJAR
SV?, B?, S	LITTLE SWIFT
PM, B?, S	PALLID SWIFT
SV, B, PM	ALPINE SWIFT
A, PM, SV, B	SWIFT
PM, C, B?	ROLLER
WV	PIED KINGFISHER
WV	SMYRNA KINGFISHER
PM, WV, R?, B?	KINGFISHER
PM, C, B?	BEE-EATER
PM, B?	BLUE-CHEEKED BEE-EATER
PM, C, WV, O, B?	HOOPOE
PM, C	WRYNECK
S, B?	SYRIAN WOODPECKER
PM, C	SAND MARTIN
PM, C, SV, B	HOUSE MARTIN
B, R?	CRAG MARTIN
A, PM, SV, C, B	SWALLOW
PM, SV, B	RED-RUMPED SWALLOW
V	DUNN'S LARK
V	DESERT LARK
V	BIFASCIATED LARK
PM, C, SV, B	SHORT-TOED LARK
PM, WV	LESSER SHORT-TOED LARK
PM, C, WV, R, B	CALANDRA LARK
PM, WV, R, B,	BIMACULATED LARK
V	BLACK LARK
R, B, C	HORNED LARK
V	TEMMINCK'S HORNED LARK
R, B, C	CRESTED LARK
R, B	WOOD LARK
PM, WV, C	SKY LARK

V	RICHARD'S PIPIT
SV, B, PM	TAWNY PIPIT
SV, B, R?	LONG-BILLED PIPIT
PM, C	TREE PIPIT
WV, C, PM	MEADOW PIPIT
PM	RED-THROATED PIPIT
PM, S	WATER PIPIT
PM, C, B?	YELLOW WAGTAIL
R, B	GREY WAGTAIL
R, B, PM, WV	WHITE WAGTAIL
PM, C, B?	RED-BACKED SHRIKE
SV, B, PM, C	MASKED SHRIKE
PM, C, SV, B	WOODCHAT SHRIKE
PM	LESSER GREY SHRIKE
PM?, Has B	GREAT GREY SHRIKE
PM, C	GOLDEN ORIOLE
V	ROSE-COLOURED STARLING
WV, C, PM	STARLING
R, B, C	JAY
V?	MAGPIE
R?	CHOUGH
R?	ALPINE CHOUGH
WV, C	JACKDAW
R, PM, C	HOODED CROW
V	ROOK
R, B	RAVEN
R, B, C	AFRICAN BULBUL
R, B	DIPPER
R, B, C	WREN
V	SIBERIAN ACCENTOR
WV?, S	DUNNOCK
R, B, C	CETTI'S WARBLER
PM, SV?, B?	SAVI'S WARBLER
V	RIVER WARBLER
V	GRASSHOPPER WARBLER
PM, B?	MOUSTACHED WARBLER
PM	SEDGE WARBLER
PM?	MARSH WARBLER
PM, SV, B?	REED WARBLER
PM, SV, B?	GREAT REED WARBLER
PM	ICTERINE WARBLER
PM, B?	OLIVE-TREE WARBLER
SV, B	UPCHER'S WARBLER

SV, B, PM, C	OLIVACEOUS WARBLER
PM?	BOOTED WARBLER
PM	BARRED WARBLER
SV, B, C, PM	ORPHEAN WARBLER
PM	GARDEN WARBLER
SV, B, PM, C, WV	BLACKCAP
PM, C, SV, B	WHITETHROAT
A, SV, B, PM	LESSER WHITETHROAT
PM, B?	RÜPPELL'S WARBLER
R, B, C, WV	SARDINIAN WARBLER
V	CYPRUS WARBLER
V, B?	MÉNÉTRIES WARBLER
V	SUBALPINE WARBLER
PM?, B?	SPECTACLED WARBLER
PM, C	WILLOW WARBLER
PM, C, WV	CHIFFCHAFF
SV, B?, PM	BONELLI'S WARBLER
PM, C	WOOD WARBLER
V	[GREEN WARBLER]
A, R, B,	GRACEFUL WARBLER
R?, B?	FAN-TAILED WARBLER
WV, V	GOLDCREST
WV, V	FIRECREST
PM, C	PIED FLYCATCHER
PM, C	COLLARED FLYCATCHER
V	RED-BREASTED FLYCATCHER
PM, C, SV, B?	SPOTTED FLYCATCHER
PM,	WHINCHAT
PM, WV, C	STONECHAT
SV, B, PM, C	WHEATEAR
PM	PIED WHEATEAR
A, SV, B, PM, C	BLACK-EARED WHEATEAR
V, B?	MOURNING WHEATEAR
PM, V	DESERT WHEATEAR
SV, B?, PM, WV	FINSCH'S WHEATEAR
PM, C, SV, B	ISABELLINE WHEATEAR
SV, B	RUFOUS BUSH ROBIN
PM, SV, B?	ROCK THRUSH
R, B, C	BLUE ROCK THRUSH
R, B, C, PM, WV?	BLACK REDSTART
PM, C, SV, B?	REDSTART
WV, C, PM	ROBIN
A, PM, B?	NIGHTINGALE

PM, C	THRUSH NIGHTINGALE
PM, WV, S	BLUETHROAT
V	RED-FLANKED BLUETAIL
SV, PM, B?, S	WHITE-THROATED ROBIN
WV	FIELDFARE
WV	REDWING
WV, S	RING OUSEL
R, B, PM, WV	BLACKBIRD
WV, PM	SONG THRUSH
WV, PM?	MISTLE THRUSH
R, B	SOMBRE TIT
R, B	COAL TIT
WV, S	BLUE TIT
R, B, C	GREAT TIT
V	NUTHATCH
R, B	NEUMAYER'S ROCK NUTHATCH
R?, B?	WALL CREEPER
WV, SV, B	PALESTINE SUNBIRD
A, R, B	HOUSE SPARROW
PM, SV, B	SPANISH SPARROW
A, R, B	ROCK SPARROW
B, R?, SV?	PALE ROCK SPARROW
PM, WV, C, R, B	CHAFFINCH
WV, S	BRAMBLING
V	RED-FRONTED or GOLD-FRONTED SERIN
R, B, C	TRISTRAM'S SERIN
WV, C	SERIN
R, B, C, WV	GREENFINCH
WV, S	SISKIN
R, B, C, WV	GOLDFINCH
R, B, C, WV	LINNET
R, B	CRIMSON-WINGED FINCH
WV, O	DESERT FINCH
R, B, S	TRUMPETER FINCH
WV	HAWFINCH
R, B, WV	CORN BUNTING
WV, S	YELLOWHAMMER
R, B	ROCK BUNTING
V, PM?, WV?	CINEREOUS BUNTING
PM, C, SV, B	ORTOLAN BUNTING
PM, C, SV, B	CRETZSCHMAR'S BUNTING
V	LITTLE BUNTING

SV, B	BLACK-HEADED BUNTING
V	REED BUNTING

EXTRAS

....

....

....

....

....

....

....

....

NOTE ON THE FOLLOWING FAMILIES:

PODICIPEDIDAE
PROCELLARIIDAE
PELECANIDAE
PHALACROCORACIDAE
ARDEIDAE
THRESKIORNITHIDAE
ANATIDAE

These families consist of water-birds which are not well represented in Lebanon, owing to the mountainous country and almost complete lack of lakes, swamps, lagoons and mudflats. Such birds of these families as occur on passage are often unrecorded because they are shot and carried off almost at once. Others are overlooked on account of the lack of any regular recording by experienced bird-watchers in the few suitable spots. On account of all these factors, this description of the birds of Lebanon gives a disproportionate amount of space to Passerine birds and birds of prey, and only the following very limited descriptions of water birds. Fuller descriptions, however, are easy to find in books of European and African birds.

LITTLE GREBE *Podiceps ruficollis.* Length 10½ in.

RANGE: It is said to breed in Lebanon as well as in Syria and Palestine, but it has little suitable habitat or safe shelter in this country though it has been seen at Ammiq Swamp in summer and autumn. It is also a winter visitor and migrant through Lebanon. Its breeding range is widespread in Africa and right across Europe and Asia except in the north.

IDENTIFICATION: A little, dark, rounded, tailless, water-bird, looking like a chick and sometimes called 'Dabchick'. It is a frequent diver. In breeding plumage it is dark brown, paler beneath, with chestnut on the cheeks and throat; in winter paler with white throat and pale neck.

NOTES: A short 'whit, whit', and a squealing, trilling note.

HABITAT: Chiefly on fresh-water lakes, where it spends a lot of time underwater, diving frequently, or it may skulk in dense vegetation along the margins. (See other Grebes, pages 12, 13 and 186.)

summer winter

CORY'S or MEDITERRANEAN SHEARWATER

Calonectris diomedea. Length 18 in.

RANGE: Breeds in the Mediterranean and on islands off Portugal and West Africa, and winters to South Africa. It may be seen off the Lebanon coast, especially in late summer and in autumn. Occasionally, at this season, a large gathering joins with Manx Shearwaters weaving to and fro offshore in pursuit of shoals of fish.

IDENTIFICATION: Cory's can be distinguished from Manx Shearwaters by their larger size, rather slower wing-movement, lighter, more grey-brown upper plumage, merging into pure white underparts without the sharply contrasting border-line along the face and neck, and by the yellow instead of blackish bill.

NOTES: Short, low notes and a long wailing one are heard from breeding places.

HABITAT: The Mediterranean in general and sometimes near the coast, flocking and feeding with the Manx. Nests in holes and crevices on wild offshore islands.

MANX SHEARWATER *Puffinus puffinus*. Length 14 in.

RANGE: At least two races of this species frequent the Mediterranean, and the eastern race, *P.p. yelkouan*, occurs off the Lebanon coast, sometimes in very large numbers in late summer and autumn.
IDENTIFICATION: The upper side is dark brown, sometimes appearing black, and the underparts are white. The name Shearwater, is descriptive of the way in which these birds fly very close to the surface of the sea, gliding alternately with a few wing-beats, and banking slowly from side to side, so that the white underparts show up intermittently.
NOTES: Weird, sepulchral croonings and crowings are chiefly heard from birds at their resting burrows.
HABITAT: When at sea, usually not very far from land, feeding in flocks on very small fish, squids, etc. The nesting holes or deep burrows are in large colonies usually on islands and rocky and turfy cliffs or slopes, sometimes in rock crevices.

GANNET *Sula bassana.* Length 36 in.

RANGE: Though largely an Atlantic bird, the handsome great Gannet, with wing-span of 6 feet, is sometimes seen off the Lebanon coast from autumn to spring, especially after gales.
IDENTIFICATION: A large white bird with long wings heavily black-tipped, and rather long, pointed white tail, and massive, forward-jutting bill. Immature plumage is dark, or, at a later stage, white with blackish blotches and flight feathers. The flight is easy, gliding and wheeling, like a gull. The bill is often pointing downward as the bird scans the sea below. Fish are caught by a headlong plunge into the water from a considerable height.
NOTES: A low, grating or rasping bark.
HABITAT: Chiefly ocean-going. Breeds in large, crowded colonies on the ledges of rocky islands.

PYGMY CORMORANT *Phalacrocorax pygmaeus*. Length 19 in.

RANGE: The breeding range of this species lies north of Lebanon, but the bird has been recorded occasionally on the Litani and other rivers flowing into the sea. The Pygmy is about half the size of the common Cormorant. The latter's breeding and feeding area is also further north and it is rarely seen in Lebanon. The Shag (a similar bird), though breeding as near as Cyprus, has not been recorded.
IDENTIFICATION: Plumage blackish with green gloss and white spots, a greyish band across back and fore-wings, and a dark red-brown head. In autumn and winter plumage the breast is red-brown, the throat white, and the white spots disappear. Immature plumage is similar to that of winter but with light or whitish underparts and yellowish bill.

The longish neck and general appearance when swimming, diving and in flight, is like that of other cormorants, but it is much smaller, with rounder head and shorter bill.
NOTES: It may croak or grunt, but no notes are known to me.
HABITAT: Chiefly rivers, marshes and lakes. Nests in colonies in marshes or bushes.

1. Cormorant, adult winter, also typical Atlantic type.

1A. Breeding, chiefly Continental type.

2. Pygmy Cormorant.

3. Shag.

LITTLE BITTERN *Ixobrychus minutus*. Length 14 in.

RANGE: Possibly breeding or attempting to do so at Ammiq Swamp. A pair appeared to be resident there as recently as May 1965. Others have been seen or shot there, and also near the coast in spring and autumn, so, presumably, it is a frequent migrant. Its main breeding areas are in parts of Asia, continental Europe, eastern Mediterranean countries, and tropical to southern Africa. It also winters in Africa.
IDENTIFICATION: The smallest of the heron family, this tiny Bittern is unmistakable with a large area of creamy-white in the wing contrasting with the blackish flight-feathers and back of the male. The female is similar, but browner, with buffish wing-patches; the immature brown and streaked. The birds are skulking and secretive.
NOTES: Croakings, and a very low, repeated, regular croak at breeding places.
HABITAT: Reed-beds, swamps with good cover, overgrown ditches and thickets by streams. (See Bittern, pages 12, 13, 187.)

NIGHT HERON *Nycticorax nycticorax*. Length 24 in.

RANGE: Though only a migrant in spring and autumn, it is seen occasionally along the coast or at the Ammiq Swamp. It may even have attempted to breed at the latter place, together with other large water-birds, but it has not found shelter or protection from shooters. The breeding range lies both north and south of Lebanon.
IDENTIFICATION: A small, short heron, looking, on the wing, almost owlish (except for the stout, pointed bill), with wide round-ended, grey wings and shortish legs. When perched, it shows white underparts, forehead and cheeks, black crown, nape and back, grey wings and tail, red eyes and a few long, drooping white plumes hanging down the black nape and back. It is a handsome, stocky bird. The immature plumage is brown, spotted with cream above, and pale beneath, streaked with brown.
NOTES: A hollow croak.
HABITAT: Swamps, marshes and river banks with plenty of thick cover and tangled shrubs and herbage. Nests in colonies, often with other herons, on trees or in bushes, or sometimes in reeds.

LITTLE EGRET *Egretta garzetta*. Length 22 in.

RANGE: Though the breeding range in Europe, Asia and Africa does not include Lebanon, the Little Egret is not uncommonly seen on migration at inland waters, rivers, and passing by out at sea.
IDENTIFICATION: A snowy white, graceful little heron, much smaller than the three following, with black bill and legs and oddly contrasting yellow feet. In breeding plumage there is a drooping crest from the back of the head and a mantle of delicate hair-like plumes. The nuptial plumes are called 'Osprey plumes' by milliners, as are similar feathers from other egrets and herons. In flight the white wings look short and rounded in comparison with those of the large herons.
NOTES: In the breeding season, there are croaks and a babbling note.
HABITAT: Shallow pools and margins of lakes, also swamps, marshes, etc. Nesting colonies may be near water, in a marsh, or high up in trees or bushes; often on the tops of stone-pines in dry country.

GREAT WHITE EGRET *Egretta alba*. Length 35 in.

RANGE: The Great White Egret or Great White Heron has only been recorded a few times at Ammiq Swamp and the coast. It has a world-wide range, the nearest part of which is probably in Turkey, and some of these birds appear to winter in Egypt.
IDENTIFICATION: It is a large, all white and very slender bird. The legs, feet and bill are blackish in summer, the bill yellow in winter. It flies like other herons.
NOTES: Sometimes croaks.
HABITAT: The banks of lakes, rivers, reed-beds.

GREY HERON *Ardea cinerea*. Length 36 in. (See under Purple Heron.)

Purple Heron. Grey Heron.

PURPLE HERON *Ardea purpurea*. Length 31 in. Page 9

RANGE: Both breed further north and west, and the Purple Heron also in Jordan, and both are seen here occasionally on passage by marshes, rivers and the coast.

IDENTIFICATION: The Grey Heron has a white head, neck and underparts with a black stripe from the bill to the thin, drooping crest and black markings down the front of the long, slender neck and shaggy upper breast. The back and wings are grey with blackish flight-feathers. Bill usually yellow. In flight the neck is withdrawn and the head sunk on the shoulders, but the feet protrude behind the tail. The flight is slow and majestic, and the great wings span 6 feet. The Purple Heron is rather smaller, darker above and russet-maroon beneath, with some drooping chestnut feathers on the mantle, and the neck is golden-chestnut. The neck- and wing-patterns and manner of flight are similar to those of the Grey Heron.

NOTES: Both species croak occasionally, or call a loud 'frank'.

White Stork.

HABITAT: The Grey Heron chiefly at lakes or streams, also reeds and marshes; the Purple Heron chiefly at reed-beds and swamps. The Grey Heron nests colonially, usually in tree-tops, the other usually colonially in reed-beds or thickets in swamps.

SQUACCO HERON *Ardeola ralloides.* Page 13

Breeds in Mediterranean countries, Asia and Africa and is recorded on passage. Seen several times in trees south of Sidon in April. Smaller than Little Egret. Sandy-buff on body, white wings and tail. Juvenile streaked with brown on body.

Family CICONIIDAE

WHITE STORK *Ciconia ciconia.* Length 40 in. Page 10

RANGE: This is a fairly common passage migrant in Lebanon, especially in spring. Great flocks of several thousand have been seen very rarely over the coast. Perhaps others pass out of sight, which would account for the scarcity of records involving large numbers. Meinertzhagen, however, gives the main migration route as passing through Syria east of Lebanon and just east of Damascus. On the east side of the Lebanon range it is not unusual to see smaller flocks of storks passing through over the plateau of Bekaa, sometimes alighting on the cultivated fields in this area. Unfortunately, some are shot, with no regard for their beneficial effects on agriculture. They feed on large numbers of grasshoppers and locusts as well as on other large insects, rodents, frogs and snakes. It breeds in north-west Africa and parts of Europe and Asia, and winters in tropical and southern Africa, Iraq and India.

IDENTIFICATION: A familiar, unmistakable, very large white bird with black flight feathers, long neck fully extended in flight, long thick red bill, and red legs and feet protruding beyond the tail. In the breeding area it may be seen standing by its enormous stick nest on many a town or country house. It is a splendid sight as it nests on roofs, towers and tall platformed posts.

NOTES: Usually quiet, but when breeding it makes noisy bill-clapping in display and as greeting to its mate, with head thrown back or drooping over the nest. It also grunts and hisses.

HABITAT: Plains, meadows, agriculture, and sometimes marshes.

BLACK STORK *Ciconia nigra.* Page 13

Breeds chiefly north and east of Lebanon. Uncommon migrant near coast in spring and autumn. Glossy back and white with red bill.

1. BITTERN. Streaky brown. Points bill upward when nervous, for camouflage in reeds, etc. (See page 187.)
2. SQUACCO HERON. (See page 9.)
3. SPOONBILL. White with dark bill. Juvenile has black on wing tips. (See page 187.)
4. FLAMINGO. Pinkish-white. Bright red on black edged-wings. Long, pink legs. (See page 187.)
5. BLACK STORK. (See page 11.)
6. CRANE. Grey with drooping plumes hiding tail. Broad white band on black head and neck. Red crown-patch, black flight-feathers. (See page 189.)
7. GREY LAG GOOSE. Grey with white near tail. Light blue-grey fore-wing in flight. (See page 187.)
8. WHITE-FRONTED GOOSE. Brownish-grey. Adult: dark blotches under body, white mask above bill. White near tail. (See pages 187, 193.)
9. WHITE PELICAN. White with black primaries. Great, long wings. Huge yellowish bill and pouch. Immature brownish. (See page 186.)
10. GREAT CRESTED GREBE. Winter: whitish, dark crown and back, strong pinkish dagger-shape bill. Summer: black and ginger 'horned' and 'frilled' head. (See page 186.)
11. BLACK-NECKED GREBE. Smaller than above. Winter: dark cap to below eye, thin dark bill. Summer: black neck, yellow plumes from cheeks. (See page 186.)
12. SHOVELER. Male: green-black head, huge bill, white breast, chestnut underneath. In flight, white on body, large pale bluish area on dark wing. Brown female also blue in wing. (See pages 188, 193.)
13. WIGEON. Male: grey back and sides, white and black to rear, chestnut head, pale crown, cinnamon breast. In flight, large patch of white on wing. Female: brown. (See pages 188, 193.)
14. GARGANEY. Male: dark head and breast, white band from eye to nape. Female: brown. (See pages 188, 193.)
15. POCHARD. Male: chestnut head, black breast, grey body and wings. Female: brownish. (See pages 188, 193.)
16. BLACK-WINGED STILT. Black and white, slender. Very long pink legs. (See pages 52, 190.)
17. AVOCET. Black and white. Thin up-curved bill, grey-blue legs. (See pages 52, 190.)
18. WHIMBREL. Brown, white rump, striped crown, down-curved bill, vibrant tittering whistle. (See page 190.)
19. SPOTTED CRAKE. (See page 51.)
20. BAILLON'S CRAKE. (See page 51.)
21. LITTLE CRAKE. (See page 51.)
22. LONG-EARED OWL. Streaked brown. Long 'ear'-tufts raised in alarm. (See pages 77, 78, 191.)
23. SHORT-EARED OWL. Streaked light brown, very dark round eyes. 'Ear'-tufts hardly visible. Hunts by day. Long wings. (See page 191.)
24. EAGLE OWL. Huge owl, sandy and cream, streaked and barred. Whitish face. Some races all brown. Long, sloping 'ear'-tufts. (See page 191.)

1.
2.
3.
4.
5.
6.
7.
8.
9.
10.
11.
12.
13.
14.
15.
16.
17.
18.
19.
20.
21.
22.
23.
24.

TEAL *Anas crecca*. Length 14 in.

RANGE: The Teal breeds widely in Europe and Asia, well north of Lebanon, and may be seen on passage on any kind of water. It is also recorded as a winter visitor and would stay on if it did not get shot. In Cyprus it is the commonest duck in mid-winter.
IDENTIFICATION: A very small duck with rapid flight. The male has a chestnut head with a wide band of bright bottle-green enclosing the eye to the nape. The back and flanks are finely vermiculated with grey, with a white streak above the wing formed by white, elongated scapulars. Beneath the tail is an area of creamy buff, divided down the centre, and also divided from the flanks by a black area. The female is streaked and spotted with brown. Both show a bright green speculum with narrow white margin in the wing.
NOTES: The Teal 'creaks' in flight and has conversational chuckling notes, quacks, squeaks, etc.
HABITAT: As Mallard.

1.

2.

1. Teal, male and female. 2. Mallard, male and female.

MALLARD *Anas platyrhynchos.* Length 23 in.

RANGE: Breeds almost throughout Europe and most parts of Asia, chiefly north of Lebanon, and travels south to a limited extent in winter. It has been recorded occasionally on passage and probably occurs regularly, though briefly on account of shooting.
IDENTIFICATION: The Mallard is a rather large bird in comparison with most other fresh-water ducks. The male has a deep, bottle-green, glossy head, a thin white collar, dark chestnut breast, light fawn back and flanks and a white tail with curled black central feathers and black hindparts. The female is streaky brown. Both have a violet speculum, white-edged, in the wing.
NOTES: Female quacks loudly like domestic ducks. Male has low 'dreek'.
HABITAT: Lakes, rivers, marshes. In winter sometimes the coast.

PINTAIL *Anas acuta.* Length 22 in. Page 193

RANGE: Breeds far north of Lebanon in Europe and Asia, but has been recorded in fair numbers as a migrant to Africa and southern Asia and a winter visitor offshore or on inland water.
IDENTIFICATION: A rather slender, long-necked duck with a thin needle-pointed tail. The upperparts of the male are grey, the underparts white, and a white stripe on each side of the neck starts at the base of the chocolate-brown head, behind the ear-coverts, and widens out to merge into the white breast. The pin-like feathers at the centre of the white tail are black, and the black hindparts are divided from the grey flanks by a wide white band. The female is streaky brown with a longer and more slender neck than that of the female Mallard, and with a pointed brown tail. Immature drakes and those in 'eclipse' are rather like the duck.
NOTES: A low whistle, quack and grunts.
HABITAT: Coastal bays, estuaries and inland water.

1. SHELDUCK. Large duck. White. Green-black head, upper neck, scapulars, primaries; dark band beneath, wide chestnut band round forepart of body. Red bill with (male) knob. (See pages 187, 193.)
2. FERRUGINOUS DUCK. Small duck. Dark red-brown, blackish back, white belly and under tail. In flight, white wing-bar. (See pages 188, 193.)
3. SANDERLING. Small, whitish, fast-running shore-bird. Winter, grey above, blackish wing bend and tip. Summer, sandy head, neck, back. (See page 190.)
4. BROAD-BILLED SANDPIPER. Smaller than No. 3. Dark in summer, Snipe-like stripes on head and back. White beneath, dark breast. Greyer in winter. Bill slightly down-curved at tip. Short legs. Shy, hides in herbage. (See page 190.)
5. GREENSHANK. Tall Wader. Streaked white head and neck. Dark wings and scapulars. Underparts, rump and centre-back white. Greenish legs. Bill slightly up-curved. (See page 190.)
6. OYSTERCATCHER. Large black and white shore-bird. Orange bill, pink legs. Striking black and white wings and tail in flight. (See page 189.)
7. RUFF. Redshank-Greenshank size. Brown. White patch each side of dark tail. Male, summer, large ruff and head tufts, yellow, rust, black or white, etc. (See page 190.)
8. REDSHANK. Less tall than Greenshank, browner, orange-red legs. In flight, white rump, wide white band rear edge of wings. (See page 190.)

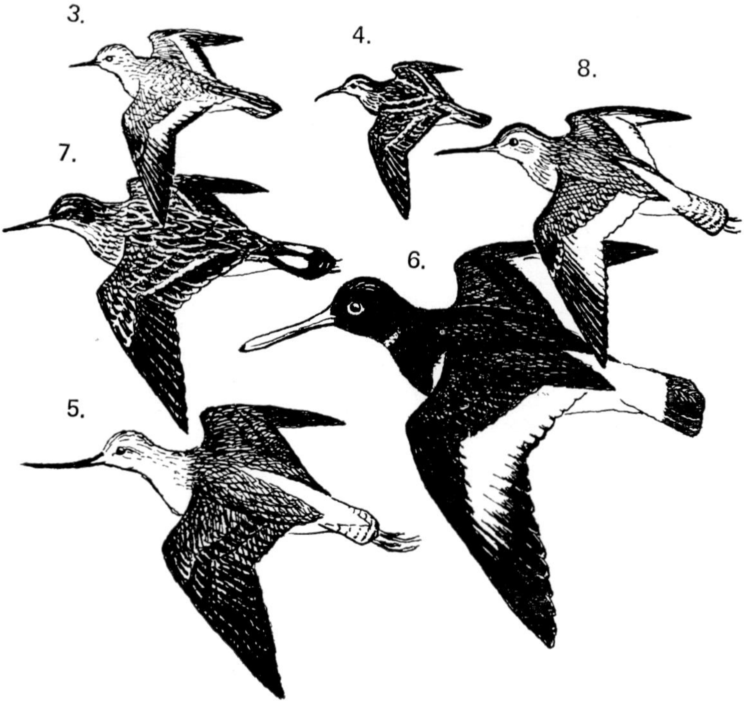

See captions opposite.

NOTE ON THE FAMILIES:

PANDIONIDAE, ACCIPITRIDAE, FALCONIDAE

The great migrations, chiefly in autumn, of birds of prey through Lebanon are one of the most interesting and spectacular features of Lebanon's ornithology. The passage here of thousands of raptors does not seem to have been reported in the older records, nor in any since then until the 1963 records were published in *Ibis* in 1967,* though a similar spectacle is well known both north and south of Lebanon. The migrations vary in altitude, and in good weather, with high pressure along the west side of the Lebanon range, where a concentration of the stream passes, the flow of eagles, buzzards and other raptors may be above the range of unaided sight, or appear as small specks, and pass unnoticed. The migration usually continues to trickle through intermittently all day, with rush-hour streams tending to build up after sunrise and before sunset.

It will be found well worthwhile to lie on one's back with a telescope or binoculars during the migrations and see what a wealth of species and numbers are on the move.

* See page xv (Cameron and Cornwallis).

Family PANDIONIDAE

OSPREY *Pandion haliaetus.*

Has world range, including parts of Mediterranean area. Some winter in the region and others migrate through, going to Africa. One recorded fishing close off shore near Sidon, April 1969 and eight in early October near Harissa. Buzzard-size but much longer wings. In flight, white beneath, black carpal-patches, fine bars on tail and flight-feathers, spotted breast. Black band from bill to nape of white, crested head. Above, dark brown. Plunges to catch fish with feet.

Family ACCIPITRIDAE

BLACK-WINGED KITE *Elanus caeruleus.*

Occasional straggler. One seen at Cedars in autumn. Hobby-size. In flight, white beneath, black primaries; above, pale grey, whitish tail, black shoulders (forewing).

1. Osprey.
2. Black-winged or Black-shouldered Kite.
3. Red Kite. (See page 20.)

HONEY BUZZARD *Pernis apivorus.* Length 20–23 in.

RANGE: The breeding range lies north of Lebanon, but though erratic on passage, this bird is often a most abundant migrant here, particularly along the coastal strip. I have seen it passing south in the second half of September in big flocks and thin trickles for several days and numbering several thousand. (See page xvi). The species winters in Africa.

IDENTIFICATION: When seen from beneath, sailing or soaring, it may be distinguished from most Buzzards by the narrower head, narrower, slightly longer tail and straighter, slightly less wide wings with usually at least two conspicuous dark bands crossing the flight-feathers. There may be dark carpal-patches contrasting with rather pale undersurface of wings, or the whole under-wing-coverts may be dark contrasting with silvery flight-feathers with dark tips and bars. The tail usually shows a wide terminal band and two bands near the base. The body plumage, too, is most variable. It may be brown above with greyish head and white beneath with dark blobs and conspicuous bars on the flanks, or barred all over the underparts, or the whole bird may be warmer, darker brown.

NOTES: High, shrill chatter and cries.

HABITAT: Usually wooded country. It soars and glides along hill-contours on passage.

BLACK KITE *Milvus migrans*. Length 22 in.

RANGE: Though apparently never abundant, this species is not uncommon in Lebanon in all seasons, though usually seen singly, passing north or south along the coast in spring or autumn. Scattered birds may be seen in the hills, but there is no record of breeding. This species has a vast range throughout Europe, Asia and Africa.
IDENTIFICATION: The plumage is dull darkish brown, not black, with pale chin and rather pale head and throat and slightly warmer-tinted underparts. The flight-feathers are black, the upper wing-coverts pale-edged. The wings are long, the tail slightly (not very noticeably) forked, the flight light and rather gull-like, the tail characteristically tilted from side to side when banking and gliding and used like a rudder. The immature plumage is a little paler, especially underneath.
NOTES: A thin, shrill, feeble whinneying scream, or an occasional chatter.
HABITAT: Ranges widely. Sometimes follows water, sometimes hills, searching for carrion or for refuse, often near towns or refuse dumps.

RED KITE *Milvus milvus*. Page 18

Not very uncommon as a migrant, but usually only one or two with other autumn raptors on passage. Slightly larger than Black Kite. Long wings and tail, latter deeply forked. Russet-red body, mantle and tail and whitish head. White patch under dark wing.

WHITE-TAILED EAGLE *Haliaeetus albicilla.* Length 27–36 in.

RANGE: Most of the breeding range lies north of Lebanon, but extends to Syria, and the bird is said to breed in Palestine. A few pass through near the Lebanon coast from time to time, and immature birds are seen occasionally with other eagles on passage. Adult birds are chiefly sedentary.
IDENTIFICATION: A great bulky eagle, with long heavy wings and a wing-span of around 8 feet.* The tail, which is rather short and wedge-shaped, and less bulky than that of the Golden Eagle, is white in adults. Immature birds are brown with dark tails.
NOTES: Higher and lower barking cries.
HABITAT: Rocky coasts and inlets and wild inland lakes. It feeds on fish, mammals, birds and carrion.

* See pages 194, 195.

A. adult. B. immature.

GOSHAWK *Accipiter gentilis*. Length 19–24 in.

RANGE: The breeding area lies north of Lebanon and the species is said to be almost sedentary except for irregular irruptions of birds seeking fresh food supplies. Many, however, do migrate south in autumn into Egypt, Palestine and elsewhere and are seen in Lebanon on passage, including a high proportion of immature birds, which I have seen once or twice in small circling groups, soaring with spread tails. (See page xv.)
IDENTIFICATION: It is like a huge version of the Sparrow Hawk with broad, rounded wings, especially when soaring, and longish tail, both finely but boldly barred beneath on silvery white. The white underparts of the body are finely barred also. The upperparts are brownish-grey, with a rather browner mantle. Immature plumage is rufous-brown, with rufous-buff beneath and very dark streaks (not bars). Flight is generally fast and at times dashing and agile in chase of prey, and the broad wings may show pointed tips instead of rounded ones when hunting and gliding.
NOTES: A mewing note and a staccato chatter.
HABITAT: Woods, conifers, hills, sometimes over mountain slopes.

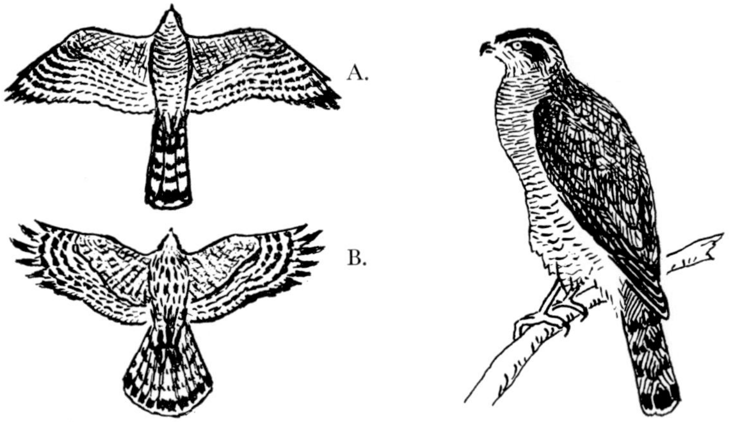

A. adult gliding. B. immature soaring.

Page 24

LEVANT SPARROW HAWK *Accipiter brevipes.* Length 13–15 in.

RANGE: The breeding range lies north of Lebanon in south-eastern Europe and western Asia. It used to breed in Lebanon and was common in summer but considerable numbers have been shot and eaten. It is seen on passage, often in large numbers, sometimes flocking like a cloud of mosquitoes high in the sky, invisible to the unaided eye.* Some winter in south Asia, in Africa and the Mediterranean area.
IDENTIFICATION: It is not always possible to distinguish between this and the Sparrow Hawk. Both have rather short, rounded wings (rather shorter in *A. nisus*) and long tails; both may look silvery from beneath with fine barring on the body and rather bolder bars on the tail, but the adult Levant Sparrow Hawk shows a very white, unbarred under-surface of the wings with contrasting blackish primary-tips, unlike the closely barred underwing of the other. Immature birds, however, show heavy blotches on the body and barred wings like *A. nisus.* The adult male is slate-blue above, the female greyish and rather larger. The male is barred with amber or rust beneath, like *A. nisus*, but it has grey cheeks instead of rufous ones, and is larger and bluer above. Females are barred beneath with dark brown on whitish.
NOTES: A shrill, double note, 'ki-vik'.
HABITAT: Open, barren country as well as woods and plantations.

SPARROW HAWK *Accipiter nisus.* Length 11–15 in.

Page 24

RANGE: The breeding area, where it is largely resident, is widespread in Europe and Asia north of Lebanon. It is doubtful if it ever bred here though early writers believed it did. However, it is seen on passage in fair numbers, wintering southward in the Mediterranean area, Asia and Africa, as well as in Europe.
IDENTIFICATION: Differs slightly from the Levant Sparrow Hawk in having a rather smaller, darker slate-blue adult male with rusty (not grey) cheeks, yellow (not dark) eyes, well barred on the under-surface of the wings, even in adults. The female is much larger and more brownish grey above and is barred beneath with dark brown on near white. See *A. brevipes* for details. Immature birds of the two species are usually indistinguishable in the field.
NOTES: Fast, repetitive, loud cries.
HABITAT: Cultivation, plantations, woods, trees anywhere.

* See pages xv, 198.

1. Levant Sparrow Hawk. 2. Sparrow Hawk.

1. Buzzard. 2. Rough-legged Buzzard.

BUZZARD *Buteo buteo*. Length 20–22 in.

ROUGH-LEGGED BUZZARD *Buteo lagopus*. Length 20–24 in.

RANGE: The Steppe Buzzard, *B.b. vulpinus*, a variety of Buzzard with a redder and sometimes darker shade of plumage than the Buzzard of Western Europe, is not uncommon in Lebanon, chiefly in autumn, winter and spring. In autumn, straggling groups are seen on passage, sometimes in very large numbers. (See page xv.) The Rough-legged Buzzard breeds in the far north and the winter hunting grounds are also chiefly north of Lebanon, but individuals are seen occasionally on passage and in winter.

IDENTIFICATION: The Buzzard is not hard to recognize when soaring round and round on upward-sloping, broad, rounded wings, often circling and gliding without flapping and with spread tail. When necessary it flaps rather slowly and heavily, or may hover on the wind or on an up-draught or (in these conditions) half fold the wings like a stout W and plunge to the ground or to a lower level like a heavy version of the Kestrel. The plumage is brown (or red-brown in this race) with a variable amount of white under the wings, on the chin and sometimes on the mottled underparts. Dark carpel patches often contrast with the silvery under-surface of the wings but are not conspicuous with dark-winged variations. The tail is usually closely barred with a wider band at the tip, but some Steppe Buzzards show only a trace of the barring on their reddish tails. The Rough-legged Buzzard is slightly larger and has a white tail with a wide, dark terminal band. It is usually whiter on the underparts and on the under-surface of the wings, with a contrasting dark carpel patch. There is a dark patch crossing the body below the pale throat and breast. The legs have pale feathers down to the feet. It hovers more frequently than the Buzzard.

NOTES: Loud, mewing calls.

HABITAT: Buzzard, wooded hills, moors, cliffs, coasts. Rough-legged Buzzard moors, marshes, bare slopes.

LONG-LEGGED BUZZARD *Buteo rufinus*. Length 24–26 in.

RANGE: This species is not uncommon here. Lebanon is situated towards the centre of its chief breeding range, and provides just the right habitat for this handsome and interesting bird. It should be given full protection from shooting which would greatly help its survival. It appears to breed in the mountains and perhaps occasionally in river valleys. It has been recorded in winter, but is seen more often on passage in early spring and autumn.
IDENTIFICATION: It is a large Buzzard with variable plumage, and rather longer, narrower tail and wings than those of the common Buzzard, the tail being unbarred in the adult (except in the very dark phase) and usually amber or pale reddish-buff. The head is often very pale, sometimes yellowish or buff streaked with brown, the upperparts red-brown mottled with brown. The underparts vary from streaked cream to red-brown with cream chin and throat, merging on the breast, and with darker thighs, or the underparts may be altogether darker. The underside of the wings looks very white with very dark primary-tips and carpel patches and pale amber, rufous or brownish wing-linings (under wing-coverts). The dark phase may look nearly black all over except for the white on the underside of the flight feathers and a pale-brown tail with dark sub-terminal band or bands. Immature birds are not unlike common Buzzards.
NOTES: A very silent bird; occasional high, mewing cries.
HABITAT: Open, rocky, barren hills and plains, ravines and wadis.

BOOTED EAGLE *Hieraaetus pennatus*. Length 18–21 in.

RANGE: The breeding area, though largely north of Lebanon, includes many Mediterranean countries and extends as far south as Palestine. In days past it was found in Lebanon, apparently as a breeding resident, but now it lacks the seclusion of woodlands and safety for breeding which it needs and is seen chiefly on passage with other raptors. (See page xv).
IDENTIFICATION: A small eagle about the size of a Kite, with rather shorter wings. There are two colour phases. The light phase is easily recognized: from beneath, when in flight, it shows a whitish body and under-wings, contrasting with blackish flight feathers. The dark phase has dark-brown underparts and under-wings. Both phases are brown above; light individuals show rufous-buff to tawny-brown on the head and neck and pale buff on the wing-coverts and upper tail-coverts, contrasting with darker flight-feathers. The dark phase has the same pattern above but with less conspicuous pale contrasts across the wings. Immature birds are rather similar to the dark phase, but more rufous. The wings are slightly tapering; the tail rather long and square cut. Though nearly buzzard-size, the bird is distinguished by longer, straighter, un-banded, light brown tail, less heavy, slightly more pointed wings and different colour-pattern. It has an extraordinarily agile, swooping flight, and is one of the most active and graceful of all birds of prey.
NOTES: A high, shrill cry, and chattering notes.
HABITAT: Forests and trees of all sorts; on passage, near the coast.

BONELLI'S EAGLE *Hieraaetus fasciatus*. Length 26–29 in.

RANGE: The breeding area includes most Mediterranean countries and Cyprus and is said to extend through the coastal regions of Syria, Lebanon and Palestine. Pairs have been reported many times, apparently breeding, in one of the river valleys on the west side of the Lebanon and a nest was recorded years ago in the Anti-Lebanon. A few are also seen with other eagles in autumn movements.

IDENTIFICATION: A moderate-sized eagle with upperparts dark brown, paler on the nape and with a white spot, whitish patch or white mottling (sometimes inconspicuous) on the centre of the back. Like the Booted Eagle, it is a rather graceful and agile bird. In flight, from beneath, it shows a very white body contrasting with long darkish wings and a longish tail with a wide dark band at the end. The under wing-coverts (under-wings) are heavily blotched with black and form a blackish area with a whitish leading edge to the wing. The white underparts of the body have some thin dark streaks or blobs, sometimes invisible at a distance. Immature birds progress from red-brown to brown, at first closely barred on the tail and secondaries. When sailing, the wings are said to slope very slightly upward, but not as distinctly so as with the sailing or soaring Golden Eagle, but it cannot be compared with the latter. Though it is larger than the (related) Booted Eagle it remains a very much slighter bird than the big *Aguila* eagles with their wide heavy wings and shortish tails.

The flight when hunting is fast and rather dashing as the bird 'stoops' on its prey.

NOTES: A fast, shrill chatter, 'kee, kee, ki-ki-ki-ki'.

HABITAT: Rocks, mountains, rocky river ravines, plains and open, lightly wooded country.

STEPPE EAGLE *Aquila rapax orientalis*. Length 25–31 in.

RANGE: Rightly or wrongly, *A. rapax*, Steppe/Tawny Eagles are here dealt with as one species. In Lebanon the race of Steppe Eagle from south-east Europe and south Russia eastward to mid-Asia, *A.r. orientalis*, is probably regular on passage and not infrequent in winter. A slightly larger race from central Asia may appear more occasionally, and perhaps a Tawny Eagle from north-east Africa, but as Tawny Eagles are largely sedentry, it is fairly clear that those seen moving south with other eagles in autumn are of the semi-migratory race of Steppe Eagles, *A.r. orientalis*. (See page xvi.)

During recent years the autumn migration of raptors through Lebanon in vast numbers has revealed a steady trickle of Steppe Eagles, chiefly in late September and October, with other eagles passing overhead in a southerly direction.

IDENTIFICATION: The Steppe Eagle migrating through Lebanon is dark brown, and in flight shows a slightly rounded tail which is closely and indistinctly barred, and a small, narrow head. The wings are wide and heavy-looking and show finger-like primary tips to blunt-ended wings, sometimes looking quite square-ended. (See page 197, flight illustrations.) It has a sluggish, gliding flight. The sandy or russet patch on the nape of the larger, eastern race, seems to be rare in *A.r. orientalis*.

Descriptions of the young by observers and writers vary considerably, but most agree that juveniles (first year birds) are pale brown to mid-brown or yellowish-brown with pale ochre to whitish wing-bars and tail-coverts above and beneath. Immature plumage is also described as rather darker brown on the body than on the wings, without the reddish tone of some Tawny Eagles. In flight this plumage may show a broad, dappled (probably varying) buff area or broad band along the front half of the wing on the median coverts and the edges of the lesser coverts, with a conspicuous, narrow whitish band behind it, formed by pale tips to the greater coverts. The secondaries are also tipped buff-white along the rear edge of the wing, and the whitish upper tail-coverts show as a wide white bar across the base of the tail. Danish literature: *Field Identification of Aquila-Eagles*, shows a pale area in two lobes or joined in one at the base and tips of the inner primaries. As the bird progresses towards maturity this pale area on the primaries is lost and the coverts become darker. (See References: Christensen, Nielsen 1968.)

NOTES: Sometimes a high-pitched 'how, how, how', but usually silent here on passage.

HABITAT: Plains and open country. In Lebanon usually migrating above the western slopes of the mountains within sight of the coast-line.

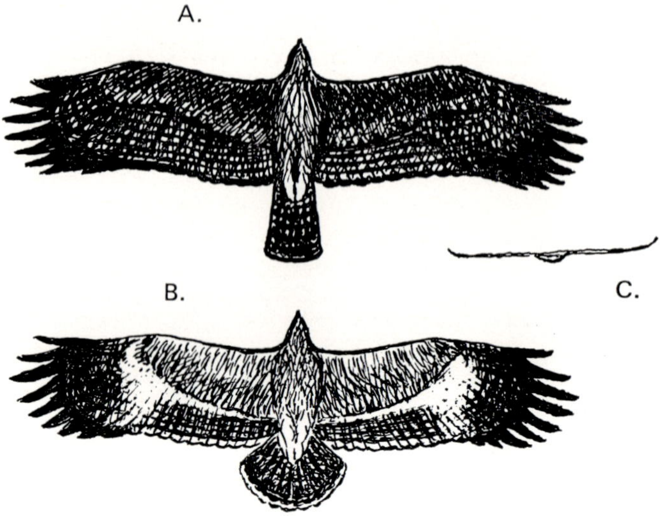

Steppe Eagle. A. adult. B. juvenile. C. sailing position.

1. Lesser Spotted Eagle, immature.
1A. sailing position.

2. Spotted Eagle, immature.
2A. sailing position.
2B. from above.

See flight illustrations, pages 195, 197, and adult Spotted Eagle, page 65.

SPOTTED EAGLE *Aquila clanga*. Length 26–29 in.

RANGE: Apparently the two Spotted Eagles are not seen in any numbers in Lebanon except on passage. Their breeding ranges lie to the north. But in autumn, especially, they may sometimes be seen passing over in hundreds and in thousands, going south, accompanied by other eagles and hawks. On these migrations *A. pomarina* appears to be the more abundant of the two.
IDENTIFICATION: Very dark brown, often appearing bronze-black, with some white on the upper and under tail-coverts. In flight it shows wide, heavy wings, short, rounded tail, small head, and sluggish flight, and may be confused with Steppe or dark Tawny Eagles; however, it has a diagnostic sailing-position with slightly downcurved wings, sometimes giving a 'partridge-look'. The juvenile plumage shows large pale buff or whitish spots or blotches on the back, scapulars, wing-coverts and the tips of the secondaries, and the upper tail-coverts are broadly tipped with white, forming a bar at the base of the tail. First year birds are sometimes so closely spotted with large whitish blotches as to appear dappled white all over the back and coverts, especially when seen in flight. Actually, the spots are small and narrow near the front edge of the wing, increasing in size to the median and greater coverts. As the young bird progresses towards maturity in the fifth year the spots on the plumage diminish. Typically, during this time, the most conspicuous white spots are reduced to two long lines on the tips of the greater and median coverts, forming two (or one) distinct wing-bars above, in addition to a narrow white fringe to the trailing edge of the wing, plus a white V at the base of the tail on the tail coverts. The underwing coverts are seen in flight to be darker than the flight feathers, while the under-wing of *A. pomarina* has the reverse pattern.
NOTES: A loud, high, yapping 'yak, yak, yak'.
HABITAT: Near water, trees, forests, marshes. In Lebanon on passage with other eagles high over the mountain slopes.

See pages xv–xvi.

LESSER SPOTTED EAGLE *Aquila pomarina*. Length 24–26 in.

RANGE: See Spotted Eagle.
IDENTIFICATION: Distinctly lighter brown than the adult Spotted and Steppe Eagles, especially on the head, neck, scapulars, wing-coverts and underparts. It is slightly smaller and less sturdy than the Spotted Eagle set and usually sails with the wings more level except for a slight dip near the tips. Its flight is lighter, more airy. It has slightly less wide, proportionately longer wings, showing extra widely-spread primary-tips when soaring, rather larger tail and more projecting, pointed head. The immature plumage shows fewer and smaller white blotches than with the Spotted Eagle, but it also has white tips to the secondaries and greater wing-coverts and small spots on other coverts, and some white on the tail-coverts; also a sandy collar at the nape, and the under wing-coverts are very pale or buff, paler than the secondaries.
NOTES: A rather shriller cry than that of the Spotted Eagle.
HABITAT: As Spotted Eagle. (See pages xv–xvi and flight illustrations, pages 195, 197.)

Page 34

GOLDEN EAGLE *Aquila chrysaetos*. Length 30–35 in.

RANGE: The southern limit of the breeding range of the Golden Eagle, which is almost entirely sedentary in its habits, includes Syria, Lebanon and Palestine, but perhaps it is not so often seen in any numbers in Lebanon as is the migratory Imperial Eagle. All visiting or resident birds of prey in Lebanon are in urgent need of protection from shooters. The Golden Eagle may still attempt to breed in the least populated mountains but this is doubtful.
IDENTIFICATION: The Golden Eagle, in some characteristics, resembles a huge buzzard, gliding, soaring with wings raised in a shallow V-shape, with up-curving primaries, and full tail. The plumage is rich, dark brown with a golden tint on the head and nape. Immature birds have more than half the tail white, ended with a broad, dark band, and the wings show a larger or smaller area of white at the base of the primaries. The white diminishes as maturity progresses but at all ages this species tends to show whitish spots where pale feather-bases come to light.
NOTES: Usually a single yap or mewing note.
HABITAT: Frequents mountains and cliffs and chiefly deforested country.

IMPERIAL EAGLE *Aquila heliaca*. Length 31–33 in. Page 34

RANGE: Breeds in Cyprus, but most of its range lies further north. In former years it is said to have bred here as well.
IDENTIFICATION: Blackish-brown plumage with a conspicuous pale yellowish nape and sides of crown and usually some large white blotches on the scapulars. In flight these blotches may be seen as a white oblong patch on each side of the body at the base of the wings above, or they may be inconspicuous. Immature plumage progresses from very pale tawny brown, strongly streaked below (with darker tail and blackish wing-tips), to dark, mottled brown. The wings are straight and level when sailing and the tail rather square-ended, less rounded and full than that of the Golden Eagle. (See flight illustration, pages 195, 197.)
NOTES: Barking notes.
HABITAT: Haunts lightly wooded country, plains and marshes except on migration when many species travel together following landmarks such as mountain ranges, rivers, coast-lines, etc.

1. Golden Eagle, adult.
1A. immature from beneath, soaring.

2 and 2A. Imperial Eagle, above.
2B. immature.
2C. sailing position.

Griffon Vulture. A. above. B. beneath.

GRIFFON VULTURE *Gyps fulvus*. Length 38–41 in.

RANGE: In Lebanon it is chiefly seen soaring along the mountain ridges and is not uncommon at high altitudes, where it may attempt breeding in inaccessible cliffs or crags. Usually it appears, often several together, with the flocks of raptors on autumn migration. The breeding range includes many Mediterranean countries eastward into Asia.
IDENTIFICATION: The Griffon and Black Vultures are recognized by their large size and great wings, wide, straight and long, with primaries spread like fingers. The wing-span is at least 9 feet. In flight, the silhouette of each is distinctive. The Griffon has a very short, squarish tail. Pale areas under the dark wings follow wing-bone structure. The plumage above is sandy grey-brown with buff on wing-coverts and with blackish flight-feathers and tail. The ruff is pale or whitish, brownish in juvenile, the head and neck thinly covered in greyish-white down. The long, snaky neck is withdrawn in flight and only the small, narrow head emerges from the ruff.
NOTES: Usually silent; croaking or whistling sounds are heard in the breeding season.
HABITAT: Mountains and plains. Nests on precipice ledges or in caverns.

CINEREOUS or BLACK VULTURE *Aegypius monachus*. Length 39–42 in.

RANGE: Mediterranean countries eastward. Only seen occasionally, though one or two may occur with Griffons in seasonal movements. It usually prefers more wooded slopes, nesting on trees.
IDENTIFICATION: Differs from the Griffon Vulture in having a rather longer, slightly wedge-shaped tail and darker plumage appearing black all over, though it is really very dark brown, with pale-brown to blackish ruff round the skinny neck which is scantily covered in fur-like blackish or brown down, with thicker tufts on the head. For general characteristics and notes, see above.

EGYPTIAN VULTURE *Neophron percnopterus*. Length 23–26 in.

RANGE: Perhaps the most familiar vulture in Lebanon, though by no means numerous. A few appear to live in the mountains and are said to breed in inaccessible places. It is also present in winter, but is seen most frequently in spring and autumn movements, many birds being in immature plumage. (See page xv.) The breeding range includes the Mediterranean countries and south in south-west Asia.
IDENTIFICATION: A large, thick-set bird of prey with white plumage and black-ended and black-fringed wings which are more tapering than those of the much larger Black and Griffon vultures. The pointed, wedge-shaped tail is white. Immature plumage varies from brown to mottled, dirty white, with brownish-white, always characteristic pointed wedge tail. The bare, skinny featherless face and throat is yellow in the adult and dirty-greyish in the immature, with a creamy-buffish hood or ruff.
NOTES: A very silent bird. Only rarely a hiss, grunt or mew has been recorded.
HABITAT: Ranges anywhere, but preferably in open country, in search of food, usually carrion or garbage. Will join other vultures devouring a carcass, but prefers excrement.

A. adult. B. immature.

SHORT-TOED EAGLE *Circaetus gallicus*. Length 25–27 in.

RANGE: Breeds in Asia and the Mediterranean countries. It is not uncommon in the Lebanon on passage in spring and autumn and also apparently breeding. (See page xv.) It is a fine bird needing more encouragement and protection. It feeds almost entirely on reptiles and hunts in the mountains at no great altitude.

IDENTIFICATION: Grey-brown above with blackish wing-tips. From beneath, the body and very long, straight wings show pure white except for a few spots or faint bars and the dark primary-tips, and with most individuals (not all) a contrasting dark bib. The longish tail shows faint bars, and a wider one at the tip. Juvenile plumage is more rufous-buff beneath, but immature plumage is variable: sometimes described as very pale, white, buff or brownish beneath. In sailing and soaring the wings are straight and level, in hovering, which is common, they are usually kinked or slightly bent back to the W-position, often with drooping legs.

NOTES: A mewing, plaintive note and others.

HABITAT: Chiefly in mountains and rocky gorges, but also over plains and woods.

PALLID HARRIER *Circus macrourus*. Length 17–19 in.

RANGE: The breeding areas of all three Harriers lie north of Lebanon, the Pallid in Asia, the Montagu's chiefly in mid Europe and mid to west Asia, and the Hen Harrier in mid to north Europe and Asia. All three pass through Lebanon on passage, and the Pallid Harrier is a not uncommon migrant in spring and autumn. The other two are occasional on passage and the Hen Harrier has been recorded two or three times near Ammiq Swamp in winter.
IDENTIFICATION: The adult male plumage of all three Harriers is pale grey with blackish wing-tips, but the Pallid is the palest, with an almost white head and pure white underparts. Females of all three are brown above, paler with streaks below, white on the rump, and are difficult to distinguish from one another. The immature Pallid Harrier has unstreaked rufous underparts.
NOTES: All three Harriers have high, chattering notes.
HABITAT: Moors, marshes, plains and hills.

MONTAGU'S HARRIER *Circus pygargus*. Length 16–18 in.

Male distinguished from Pallid Harrier by grey breast and white belly streaked with rufous-brown. The wing shows at least one narrow black bar across the secondaries. Female and immature birds are as Pallid Harrier.

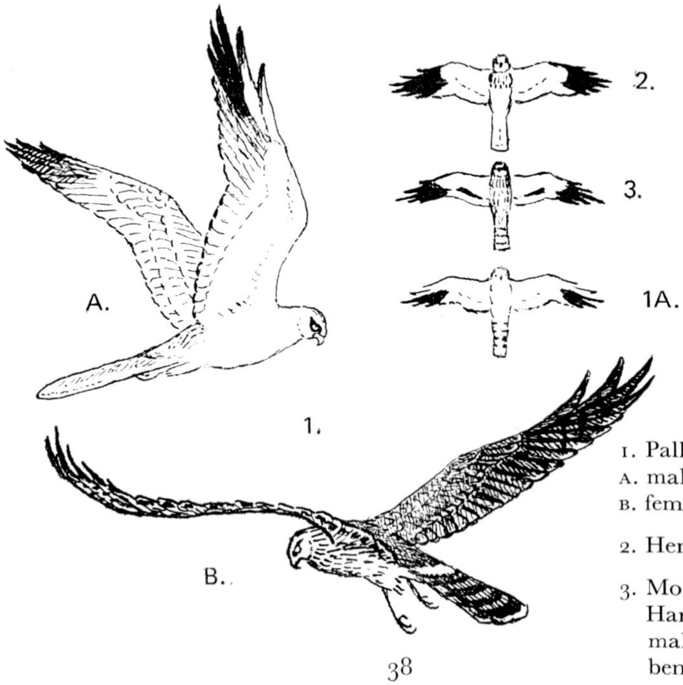

1. Pallid Harrier.
A. male.
B. female.

2. Hen Harrier.

3. Montagu's Harrier, males from beneath.

HEN HARRIER *Circus cyaneus*. Length 17–20 in.

Male distinguished from Pallid Harrier by light grey breast, white belly and pure white rump. Female distinguished by having a little more white on the rump than the preceding two, and by being a little larger and more robust. Immature birds are streaky brown like females.

MARSH HARRIER *Circus aeruginosus*. Length 19–22 in.

RANGE: Palestine appears to be the southern limit of the breeding range, which covers a large area of Europe and Asia. Marsh Harriers have often bred or attempted to do so in Ammiq Swamp, where they have also been seen in winter. They are also seen on migration.
IDENTIFICATION: Harriers have long wings, more slender than buzzards' or hawks', and rather long, straight, narrow tails. The Marsh Harrier is the largest and most bulky of those which visit Lebanon, and is extremely variable in appearance. It may be seen skimming rather slowly, low over a reed bed or marsh with wings stiffly raised, seldom level, scanning the ground for frogs or other prey. The adult male has grey secondaries and tail, black wing-tips, pale, yellowish, streaked head and breast and brown mantle. Younger males and females are variable chocolate-brown with buff or cream crown, nape, chin and 'shoulders', old females being nearly white-capped. Some are all dark.
NOTES: A thin, double, squeaky cry.
HABITAT: Swamps, marshes, reed-beds, and, on passage, near the coast above mountain slopes, in company with other migrants.

A. male from beneath. B. from above. C. female and immature.

Family FALCONIDAE

LANNER *Falco biamicus*. Length 15–18 in.

RANGE: Lebanon lies nearly at the northern limit of the Lanner's breeding range through Africa and the Mediterranean countries, and nesting places are unknown here in recent years, though the birds have been recorded in the breeding season.
IDENTIFICATION: Female (the larger) like a brownish-grey peregrine with a sandy or golden-buff cap and nape and a narrow dark moustachial stripe. The underparts are whitish with some dark spots (unbarred). Immature more heavily streaked beneath. Adult male is more slate-grey above.
NOTES: Short, shrill cries, usually in the breeding season.
HABITAT: Mountain ravines, cliffs, ruins, barren wastes and rocks.

SAKER *Falco cherrug*. Length 16–20 in.

RANGE: The Saker has been recorded only occasionally, but it is a fairly common migrant and winter visitor in Cyprus and may pass largely unnoticed here. Its main breeding area lies north and east, but migrants pass through to Arabia and north-east Africa and some also winter in the Levant.
IDENTIFICATION: The Saker is very large, grey-brown above with pale amber or rusty feather edgings, and white beneath and on the head and neck, speckled and streaked with brown, and has only thin, faint moustache-lines. Immature plumage is much more heavily streaked beneath and tends to be darker and browner.
HABITAT: Chiefly plains and deserts.

1. Lanner. 2. Saker. 3. Peregrine. 4. Eleonora's Falcon.

PEREGRINE *Falco peregrinus*. Length 15–19 in.

RANGE: Lebanon is in the Peregrine's almost world-wide breeding range. The smaller race, *F.p. brookei*, known as the Lesser Peregrine breeds in parts of the Levant. Maybe it once bred here, but proof is wanting, at least in recent years. It is chiefly seen in spring and autumn. It is not clear where to draw a line between the range of this and the Barbary Falcon, *F. pelegrinoides*, of North Africa and Arabia which seems to be regular in Jordan, probably breeding, and doubtless occurs here. (See page 202.)
IDENTIFICATION: The Peregrine is like a giant Hobby, but the whitish underparts of the adult are barred (not streaked), the moustachial lobe is wider and there is no rufous below. The flight is fast and strong and the 'stoop' dashing. Like many of the falcons, the female is considerably larger than the male. Immature plumage is browner in tone, heavily streaked (not barred) beneath on the buff underparts.
NOTES: Various cries including a sharp 'kek-kek-kek'.
HABITAT: Mountains, cliffs, rocky ravines, marshes.

ELEONORA'S FALCON *Falco eleonorae*. Length 15 in.

RANGE: The scarce Eleonora's Falcon breeds on rocky islands in the Mediterranean, including Cyprus, and has been recorded several times in Lebanon. It is most likely on passage, as in winter it migrates to the coast of East Africa, and I have seen it at sea off the coast of Egypt in autumn.
IDENTIFICATION: Not quite as large as the Peregrine, and more slender. It has two phases: one is dark grey-brown above and densely streaked below on buff underparts (not barred) and looks rather like a smaller version of the immature Peregrine. The other is nearly black all over. Immature plumage is browner in tone.
NOTES: A harsh 'qui-er'.
HABITAT: Chiefly rocky islands and sea cliffs.

HOBBY *Falco subbuteo*. Length 12–14 in.

RANGE: This attractive little falcon may be the most frequently noticed bird of prey in the Lebanon hills. It breeds, when permitted by huntsmen, in some higher mountain pines and cedars and is also seen on spring and autumn migration. It breeds widely in Europe, Asia and Mediterranean countries, including Cyprus.
IDENTIFICATION: Upperparts dark slate grey, head, cheeks and moustachial stripe nearly black, throat and sides of neck white, underparts creamy buff with heavy blackish streaks, forming dense stripes, thighs and under the tail orange-rufous. The immature plumage is a little darker and lacks rufous. The flight is fast, the wings long and pointed. Beneath, in flight, it shows finely barred tail and wings and streaked body.
NOTES: Shrill 'ki-ki-ki-ki', and similar single cries.
HABITAT: Woods, heath-land, country with trees, and, in Lebanon, the mountain pines.

Hobby. Merlin.

MERLIN *Falco columbarius.* Length $10\frac{1}{2}$–13 in.

RANGE: This small falcon breeds widely in north Europe and north and mid-Asia and is sometimes recorded here on passage and also in winter.
IDENTIFICATION: The dashing little Merlin is usually seen singly. Male, above, slate-blue, female dark brown, both heavily streaked beneath. The male's streaks are on rufous-buff underparts, the female's on creamy white.
NOTES: A fast shrill chatter, other chattering cries and plaintive calls.
HABITAT: Moorlands, hills, marshes, and the coast.

RED-FOOTED FALCON *Falco vespertinus.* Length 12 in.

RANGE: The breeding range is from eastern Europe through Asia, far north of Lebanon. Here it is recorded on passage.
IDENTIFICATION: Gregarious, often seen in flocks or a few together, sometimes hawking for insects or hovering like Kestrels. It tends to be sluggish. The male is dark grey, often looking blackish with grey wings, and has orange-scarlet legs, eye-patches and bill with dark tip, and bright chestnut thighs and under tail-coverts. The female has orange-rufous crown and nape, dark patch round eye and 'moustaches', sandy-buff underparts, closely barred grey mantle and tail and scarlet legs. The young bird is similar, but browner, with pale forehead, streaked, creamy underparts and yellow legs. It is distinguished from female and young Kestrels by conspicuous, short, dark 'moustache' and shorter tail (about the length of folded wing) usually greyer and uniformly barred to tip; also, usually, by being greyer in general, less chestnut in tone.
NOTES: A high, shrill 'ki-ki-ki-ki'.
HABITAT: Plains and open country.

Red-footed Falcon. A. male. B. female.

1. Kestrel, male. 1A. female. 2. Lesser Kestrel, male.

KESTREL *Falco tinnunculus*. Length $13\frac{1}{2}$ in.

LESSER KESTREL *Falco naumanni*. Length 12 in.

RANGE: The Kestrel has a wide breeding range and nests here chiefly in the mountains, including the higher parts. It may be seen all the year round and would be much more common were it not shot and eaten at all seasons. Lebanon lies on the southern limit of the main breeding area of the gregarious Lesser Kestrel which is even more scarce here than the Kestrel. It is probably unable to establish itself in the face of persecution as its habitat is often near human habitations. Nesting colonies are generally in cliffs, quarries or rocks. It appears to be a little more plentiful in northern Lebanon than elsewhere.

IDENTIFICATION: Both have a distinctive habit of hovering, especially the Kestrel, which often hovers nearly motionless for long spells on level wings, body and tail. It is usually solitary, while the Lesser Kestrel is more often seen in twos and threes and larger parties, especially at nesting colonies.

The male Kestrel is chestnut above spotted with black and has a grey head, rump and tail, the tail having a black band at the end, tipped with white. The female is all chestnut above (except for some grey on rump), barred from head to tail. Both have speckled, streaked buff underparts, thin moustachial streaks and dark wing-tips. Immature plumage is like the female's, but more heavily barred and usually without any grey.

The Lesser Kestrel is similar but the bright chestnut of the male above is unspotted and the grey of the head and tail looks bluer and brighter and the underside of the wings and tail is whiter. A large slate-blue patch on the secondaries may show above as it skims about catching insects. Female and immature plumage is as Kestrel.

NOTES: (both) Sharp 'kik-kik-kik' and similar cries.

HABITAT: The Kestrel occurs anywhere; the Lesser Kestrel prefers open places and foothills.

CHUKAR PARTRIDGE *Alectoris chukar*. Length 13–13½ in.

RANGE: A resident in the Lebanon mountains as well as on the eastern borders of southern Europe and right across Asia. In spite of the heavy toll taken by shooting, it breeds usually in the high mountains and is not uncommonly seen in flocks after the breeding season. By many authors, this species is treated as conspecific with the Rock Partridge of Europe, *A. graeca*.
IDENTIFICATION: A compact, typical partridge, with red bill and legs, grey-brown tinted sandy above with greyish rump and buff-white throat bordered by black bib-line, buff underparts, white flanks boldly barred black and chestnut, often tinted with blue-grey on the upper breast, forehead and nape.
NOTES: Low clucking sounds or cackles hard to describe but often like domestic fowl, and unlike those of the Rock Partridge. They often include the call 'Chukar'. 'The noisy call "tok-tok-tok-tok-tok" can be heard long before the birds are seen. They also emit a "pes-chu" call.' (Moor and Boswell.)
HABITAT: Rocky mountain slopes, sides of steep ravines and desert wastes.

QUAIL *Coturnix coturnix*. Length 7 in.

RANGE: Though a summer visitor to Lebanon where it has attempted to breed in times past in the Bekaa and elsewhere, the times when the Quail is to be seen and shot in large numbers are during the massive spring and autumn migrations to and from its winter quarters in Africa and southern Asia. A few appear to linger in Lebanon in winter.

IDENTIFICATION: A small, rounded bird with low flight, and whirring wings, preferring to hide or run in cover rather than fly except on passage. The plumage is sandy-brown and covered with pale and dark streaks. The male has some black bands on the throat.

NOTES: The Quail is more often heard than seen, and the clear, liquid though quiet call, 'whit-wi-whit', generally repeated, carries for a surprising distance with ventriloquial effect.

HABITAT: Long grass, rough herbage, crops, etc.

HOUBARA *Chlamydotis undulata*. Length 25 in.

RANGE: A breeding bird of the Syrian desert, at the back door of Lebanon, and once common in Jordan and Arabia, yet we only have a few records here. *C.u. macqueenii* is the Asian race of Houbara as distinct from the African races which are rather smaller and darker.
IDENTIFICATION: A handsome bird, in size between the Great and Little Bustards, varying according to sex. The plumage is pale sandy brown, finely barred or vermiculated with black above and barred on the rufous-sandy tail; and white beneath, with some long grey feathers at the base of the neck. There are long, drooping black and white feathers which can be puffed out on each side of the neck, and a short black and white crest. In flight it lacks the very large areas of white in the wing shown by the Great and Little Bustards. The flight-feathers are black with a conspicuous white patch on the fore-wing near the end only, and pale grey greater wing-coverts form a long wing-bar between the black flight-feathers and the sandy light-brown mantle.
HABITAT: Semi-desert, barren, stony and sandy plains; sometimes in crops. (See other Bustards, page 189.)

With acknowledgements to P. J. Stead and British Birds *on flight sketches of Houbaras.*

WATER RAIL *Rallus aquaticus*. Length 11 in.

RANGE: Lebanon is within the breeding area in Europe and Asia of this shy secretive bird, but there are no nesting records, though it has been seen at Ammiq Swamp in autumn and I have heard many each spring calling in the swamp. Other records seem to be chiefly of autumn and winter migrants and visitors to other places in Lebanon.

IDENTIFICATION: Upper plumage dark chestnut-brown streaked with black, the face and underparts slate grey, flanks boldly barred black and white, abdomen buff shading to nearly white under the tail. The rather long, straight bill is red. The habits are nervous and skulking and the bird usually remains out of sight or dashes for cover when disturbed.

NOTES: This species is more usually heard than seen. It starts with a squealing like a pig, followed by a wailing groan, dying away. There is also a repeated 'jip'.

HABITAT: Reeds, thick water-side herbage, overgrown ditches etc.

CORNCRAKE *Crex crex*. Length 10½ in.

RANGE: The wide breeding range in Europe and Asia lies north of Lebanon. A few winter around the Mediterranean but most pass into Africa and are seen on passage here in spring and autumn, dropping into cover in all kinds of unsuitable places, even in Beirut, on their way. With them I have glimpsed other, smaller crakes. As far as I could see, these were Spotted, and Little Crakes, and presumably Baillons Crake which also passes on migration. All these are seen on passage through Cyprus, especially the Little Crake which is common there and often abundant.
IDENTIFICATION: Light sandy brown above with dark spots and streaks, pale beneath with chestnut barring on the flanks and under the tail. The sides of the head, neck and breast are pale grey and the ear-coverts chestnut. In flight, large areas of chestnut show in the wings and the longish legs droop behind the short tail, but the bird gives little time for examination, and drops into cover when disturbed.
NOTES: The bird is silent on passage. Only in the breeding season the harsh 'crek-crek, crek-crek', is heard.
HABITAT: Long grass, crops, herbage, etc.

Moorhen. Coot. Corncrake.

SPOTTED CRAKE *Porzana porzana.* Page 13
Probably not uncommon on migration. A few records, including two at Ammiq Swamp in April 1969. Winters in Mediterranean area. Streaked brown. Barred flanks, small white spots on head to breast, yellow under tail.

[LITTLE CRAKE *Porzana parva.*] Page 13
Winters around the Mediterranean but not yet quite positively identified in Lebanon, though abundant on passage in Cyprus. Streaked brown, grey beneath from bill downward, barred under tail. Female all brownish.

[BAILLON'S CRAKE *Porzana pusilla.*] Page 13
Seen on passage through Syria and breeds in Jordan but not yet certainly recorded here. As male Little Crake but barred on flanks. Pale tan legs, not green as Little Crake.

MOORHEN *Gallinula chloropus.* Length 13 in.

RANGE: Lebanon is within the breeding range of the Moorhen, but the only swamp offering suitable habitat is too much shot over to encourage it. It appears to be hanging on as a resident at Ammiq Swamp. I saw one there as recently as May 1965 with two small chicks. Others are recorded as migrants or in winter.
IDENTIFICATION: It spends much of its time dabbling about in the shelter of water plants, but when seen on open water it jerks its head rythmically as it swims. The plumage is dark, looking nearly black; the blackish-grey flanks are fringed with white, and the white under the tail is very conspicuous as the bird habitually flicks it up, both on land and water. The bill is red, yellow-tipped, the large feet greenish. Immature birds are dull brownish with greenish bills.
NOTES: Loud calls, a ringing, gutteral 'fullok', a harsh 'krark', and others. Habitat as above.

COOT *Fulica atra.* Length 15 in.

RANGE: The Coot has a wide breeding range in Europe and Asia. It may have bred in Anti-Lebanon, but both Coot and Moorhen are chiefly recorded as migrants and winter residents.
IDENTIFICATION: Rather similar to the Moorhen but larger, with a conspicuous white forehead-shield and bill. The plumage is grey-black, browner with immature birds, which are whitish on the throat and upper breast. The very large, greenish feet have lobed webbing round each toe. Like the Moorhen it rises from the water heavily, leaving a wake behind it as it beats the surface with its feet.
NOTES: A metallic 'Kwok', explosive 'stik', etc.
HABITAT: Lakes and other fresh water, swamps, reed-beds.

NOTE ON THE FAMILIES:
CHARADRIIDAE AND HAEMATOPODIDAE

The records of waders in Lebanon are very scanty considering the great migrations which take place in the Levant. No doubt the reason is chiefly lack of mud which is the favourite habitat of most of them, and a scarcity of inland water and marsh. Also, probably most of the waders which occur go unrecorded through lack of regular watching at all possible places, and others are shot and disappear in the early mornings, so that the following description of waders in Lebanon may not do justice to the facts.

1. Dunlin.
2. Little Stint.
3. Temminck's Stint.
4. Common Sandpiper.
5. Curlew Sandpiper.
6. Dotterel.
7. Knot.
8. Avocet.
9. Black-winged Stilt.
10. Lapwing.

(See other waders in flight, page 17.)

RINGED PLOVER *Charadrius hiaticula*. Length $7\frac{1}{2}$ in.

LITTLE RINGED PLOVER *Charadrius dubius*. Length 6 in.

RANGE: Both are known in Lebanon as not uncommon spring migrants, summer stragglers and occasional in autumn. The breeding range of the Ringed Plover lies far north, but the other breeds round the Mediterranean, though it is not recorded as doing so in Lebanon.
IDENTIFICATION: Both are small plovers, plain brown above, with white beneath, usually running nimbly along the shore or by inland waters or shingly river-beds. The Ringed Plover is the larger and, like the Little Ringed, has a narrow black bib or upper breast band. It has orange-yellow legs and orange bill with a black tip. The legs of the Little Ringed are flesh-colour to yellowish. Care is needed in identifying immature autumn migrants of these two species with brownish, interrupted breast bands which show at the sides only and may cause confusion with the Kentish Plover. The Little Ringed has no white wing-bar which is shown by the other two in flight.
NOTES: Ringed, a plaintive 'too-eet', Little Ringed, a sharp 'teeu'. Both trill in song.
HABITAT: As under 'Identification'.

KENTISH PLOVER *Charadrius alexandrinus*. Pages 54, 64
Length $6\frac{1}{4}$ in.

RANGE: Breeds around the Mediterranean and in Jordan, but in Lebanon breeding is not proved though the species is seen in spring, probably on passage only.
IDENTIFICATION: Though similar to the above species, the Kentish Plover, has only a short blackish mark on each side of the upper breast, and blackish legs and bill.
NOTES: A high, shrill 'po-eet', and soft purring 'peerrr'. It trills in song.
HABITAT: As Ringed Plover.

GREATER SAND PLOVER *Charadrius leschenaultii*. Page 64

Several were shot near Beirut last century. One or two unconfirmed records more recently, and in April 1969 two seen on 24th, four on 25th on the shore near Sidon. Probably not very uncommon on migration. It breeds in Jordan. About Dotterel-size, but with longer, heavier black bill, light ash-grey mantle and white underparts. Breeding male as shown on Plate 1. Female not unlike winter male (shown), and juveniles slightly dappled with pale buff.

Ringed Plover. Little Ringed Plover. Kentish Plover.

A. B.

Grey Plover. A. summer. B. winter.

DOTTEREL *Eudromias morinellus*. Length 8½ in.

RANGE: A mountain Plover, only seen occasionally on passage in the Bekaa and near the sea. The breeding area lies away to the north.
IDENTIFICATION: Easily recognized in spring with a white pectoral band separating the grey-brown upper breast from the rich chestnut and black underparts. The throat and a band over the eye to the nape are white, contrasting with the dark cap. In winter or immature plumage, as seen in autumn migrants, the upper parts and breast are ash-brown and the underparts become increasingly white, while the white pectoral band is only faintly contrasting.
NOTES: A plaintive pipe, and variations, and usually a pretty, twittering trill.
HABITAT: In winter it frequents steppes inland, on passage sometimes mud-flats or shore, and in spring and summer the high mountains.

GREY PLOVER *Pluvialis squatarola*. Length 11 in.

RANGE: Recorded a number of times along the Lebanon coast. The breeding area lies far to the north, but the winter quarters include the Mediterranean area.
IDENTIFICATION: Has striking plumage, black beneath and on the face and throat in the breeding season and very white above, especially on the head and neck, and speckled grey on the back. At other times it is light brownish-grey above and white beneath, finely dappled on the breast. In flight, even in winter, it shows a black patch under the base of the wing formed by black axillaries.
NOTES: A sweet, plaintive 'tee-oo-ee', dropping on the middle note and rising on the last one.
HABITAT: Estuaries, mud-flats and the shore.

Dotterel.

LAPWING *Vanellus vanellus*. Length 12 in. Page 52

SPUR-WINGED PLOVER *Vanellus spinosus*. Length $10\frac{1}{2}$ in.

RANGE: The Lapwing breeds north of Lebanon, right across Europe and Asia and winters as far south as north and north-east Africa. In Lebanon it is not uncommon on migration and in winter in the Bekaa or on the coast where large winter flocks have been recorded. The Spur-winged Plover breeds from Thrace and the Levant south into Africa. In Lebanon it is seen only occasionally as a passer by.
IDENTIFICATION: Lapwing: very dark irridescent green and bronze above, white beneath and on the face with a black bib, crown and long whispy crest, and chestnut under the black and white tail. In flight it looks black and white with floppy, rounded wings and erratic flight. (See page 52.) Spur-winged Plover: black crown and drooping crest, chin, throat, centre of upper breast to belly and flanks; white cheeks, sides and back of neck to sides of upper breast, also abdomen, under the tail and rump; black tail and wing-tips; sandy-brown mantle; wings sandy-brown, white and black. A striking bird with long black legs.
NOTES: Lapwing: Shrill 'pee-wit', Spur-winged Plover: a series of loud calls.
HABITAT: Grass or mud-flats, marshes, estuaries, farms, agriculture, the Spur-winged Plover usually near water. (See other Plovers, pages 189, 204.)

Lapwing. Spur-winged Plover.

GREEN SANDPIPER *Tringa ochropus.* Length 9 in.

WOOD SANDPIPER *Tringa glareola.* Length 8 in.

RANGE: Both breed right across Europe and Asia far north of Lebanon, and winter in the south of these continents, and the Green Sandpiper is often seen on passage in Lebanon and occasionally in winter. The Wood Sandpiper is seldom recorded here, though common and usually abundant on passage in other parts of the Levant, including Cyprus.

IDENTIFICATION: The Green Sandpiper in flight looks rather black and white, having very dark wings, underneath as well as above, and conspicuous white rump, underparts and tail, the last having dark bars at the end. The neck and breast are streaked with grey-brown and the dark mantle sprinkled with pale specks. The legs are greyish- or brownish-green and look dark.

The Wood Sandpiper is not quite so dark above and is silvery instead of blackish on the under sides of the wings. The upperparts are more thickly spotted with pale markings, the tail more barred with brown and it shows rather less white on the rump. The legs are greenish yellow and distinctly longer.

NOTES: Green Sandpiper, 'tlueet' and 'weet-a-weet'. Wood Sandpiper usually a sharp 'chiff-chiff-chiff' or 'chirrif'.

HABITAT: The coast, swamps and inland water, even at high altitudes.

1. Green Sandpiper. 2. Wood Sandpiper.

COMMON SANDPIPER *Tringa hypoleucos*. Length $7\frac{3}{4}$ in.

RANGE: This is the most familiar of the Sandpipers in Lebanon, as it is not uncommon on passage in spring and autumn and also seen sometimes in winter. The breeding range lies right across Europe and Asia north of Lebanon, and it winters to the south.
IDENTIFICATION: Brown above and at each side of the upper breast, and white beneath. In flight it shows whitish undersurface of wings and a long white wing-bar above. Legs light greyish-green. The bird flies low over the water with stiff wings slightly down-curved and with alternate spells of gliding and wing-flicking (vibrating) which are diagnostic of this species, as is the frequent bobbing of the head and swaying up and down of the tail.
NOTES: High, sharp 'pee-pee-pee'.
HABITAT: Boulder-strewn hill-streams, margins of lakes, river-sides, estuaries.

1. Common Sandpiper. 2. Little Stint. 3. Temminck's Stint. 4. Dunlin.
(See flight illustration, page 52.)

LITTLE STINT *Calidris minuta*. Length $5\frac{1}{4}$ in.

RANGE: Both this and the Temminck's Stint breed far north and some winter around parts of the Mediterranean and southern Asia and Africa, and are seen in Lebanon occasionally on passage. Many may be overlooked, as both species occur commonly in Cyprus, especially *C. minuta*.
IDENTIFICATION: A very small wader, often running about on shingle or mud pecking here and there busily as most waders do. Plumage white beneath and mottled sandy brown above in summer, with sandy tint on breast. In winter it is grey and white. It has black legs and bill and usually shows pale streaks ('braces') on the back in autumn immature plumage.
NOTES: A high-pitched repetition of 'tit-it-it'.
HABITAT: Chiefly estuaries and the coast on passage.

TEMMINCK'S STINT *Calidris temminckii*. Length $5\frac{1}{2}$ in.

IDENTIFICATION: Differs from Little Stint in having duller brown plumage above and across the breast in summer, and greyer in winter, with less white on the face and without 'braces'. It has paler legs and shows pure white on the outer tail-feathers in flight, but both Stints show a dark stripe down the central upper tail-coverts and tail, with white on the coverts on each side. It prefers marshes away from the water's edge. (See illustrations, pages 52, 59.)
NOTES: A pretty trill or twitter. For other details, see above.

DUNLIN *Calidris alpina*. Length 7 in. Pages 52, 59

RANGE: Breeds far north and winters in southern Asia, Africa and southern and western Europe. In Lebanon it is sometimes seen on passage.
IDENTIFICATION: The Dunlin is similar to the Stints, but larger, with longer, slightly down-curved bill. In summer it has a large black patch on the underparts and is chestnut-brown above with slight streaking on the upper breast. In winter it is greyish above and on the breast and white beneath. Legs and bill are black. The tail-pattern in flight is not unlike that of the Little Stint, but there is less white on the face and throat and no clear 'braces', marked on the back also the note is very different.
NOTES: A hoarse, shrill, unmusical squeak: 'weedge'.
HABITAT: Chiefly the coast on migration.

WOODCOCK *Scolopax rusticola*. Length $13\frac{1}{2}$ in.

RANGE: Breeds north of Lebanon, right across Europe and Asia, and winters as far south as the Mediterranean area. In Lebanon it is not infrequently met with in winter and sometimes on passage, recorded chiefly near the coast, in the A.U.B. campus, Beirut, in gardens and up river valleys and also in the region of the Bekaa, where even a few bushes or trees with undergrowth or herbage offer shelter.

IDENTIFICATION: A thick-set, much barred, handsomely tortoise-shelled, long-billed bird, very shy and keeping to cover. The upper-parts are patterned in chestnut, black and light buff, the underparts finely barred throughout with buff and brown. The forehead is buff, the crown and nape broadly barred black and orange. The long, straight bill is pinkish at the base deepening to black at the tip; the legs pinkish-grey to greyish-tan. In flight it is rather silent, springing from cover and showing much-barred, rounded wings.

NOTES: A low grunt and a sneeze-like ejaculation may be heard in this country.

HABITAT: Woods, thickets, over-grown river banks, tangled bushes near ditches.

COMMON SNIPE *Gallinago gallinago*. Length 10½ in.

RANGE: The breeding range lies both north across Europe and Asia and far south in South Africa. The winter range is also chiefly north of Lebanon. It is recorded here occasionally and is common in Cyprus in winter.
IDENTIFICATION: It is shy and secretive and gets up suddenly when disturbed from thick cover, with flurried zig-zag flight and rasping note. It has a very long, straight bill and is short-tailed and brown, heavily barred and streaked, with buff 'braces'-lines down the back, and long, dark-brown and buff stripes over the crown, through the eye and below it; whereas the bands on the crown and nape of the Woodcock run crosswise from side to side. It is much smaller than the Woodcock.
NOTES: A ripping, rasping ejaculation.
HABITAT: Marshes, swamps and ditches.

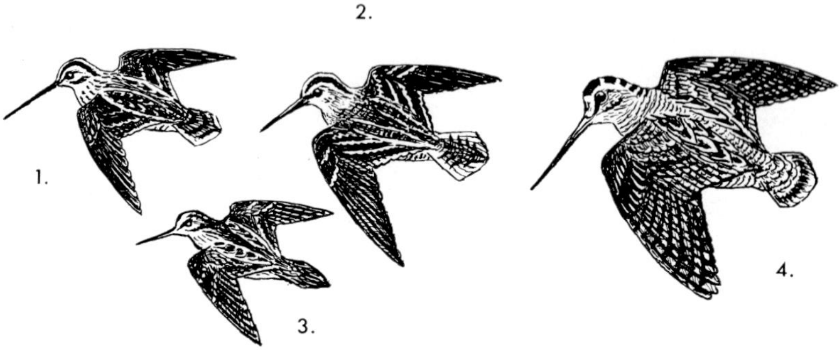

1. Common Snipe. 2. Great Snipe. 3. Jack Snipe. 4. Woodcock.

GREAT SNIPE *Gallinago media*. Length 11 in.

RANGE: Breeds far to the north and winters in Africa. It has been recorded here occasionally in winter, spring and autumn near the coast and at Ammiq Swamp, most recently at the Swamp two in April 1969.

IDENTIFICATION: It is not unlike the Common Snipe, but usually flies straighter, lower and at less speed, without the rasping cry of the other when flushed. It shows three white outer tail-feathers each side of the tail in flight, with only a few small, widely spaced, dark bars, while the Common Snipe shows only a little white at the sides of the tail. See Common Snipe for comparison.

NOTES: Sometimes a croak.

HABITAT: Marshes, swamps, ditches; also found in dry herbage and fields.

JACK SNIPE *Lymnocryptes minimus*. Length 7½ in.

RANGE: The breeding range is far north and it winters in parts of Europe, Asia and Africa. Here it occurs occasionally in winter at Ammiq and elsewhere. Perhaps it is largely overlooked.

IDENTIFICATION: A very small Snipe, getting up suddenly and silently from a ditch or marsh when disturbed, and dropping quickly into cover again. The little tail shows no white in flight and the brown plumage has conspicuous 'braces' and other pale buff stripes on the back. The bill is not so long as those of the other two Snipe.

NOTES: Usually silent in winter.

HABITAT: As Common Snipe.

SERIES 1

1. WHITE-EYED GULL. See Jordan list, page 205, and Hemprich's Gull below.

2. HEMPRICH'S or SOOTY GULL. Not unlike White-eyed Gull, but rather larger and stouter, with brown head and throat (not black), dark eye, dark brown mantle and wings (not quite so grey-brown as with White-eyed), and stouter, greenish, dark-tipped bill. The upper breast and neck are also darker than with the latter. In immature plumage very like White-eyed Gull. Hemprich's Gull is known to spread north up the Red Sea in winter, while the White-eyed (which breeds further north, and is seen at Aqaba) tends to winter to the south. (See pages 190, 205.)

3. SLENDER-BILLED GULL. Slightly larger than Black-headed Gull but with the same wing-pattern. Might be confused with the winter plumage of Black-headed, but the tail is longer and wedge-shaped, the neck and bill also longer and the head less rounded. The dark red bill and legs usually look black. Head and bill often pointing slightly downward. White parts with slight pink flush in summer. (See pages 68, 190.)

4. AUDOUIN'S GULL. Larger than foregoing, smaller than Herring Gull. (See pages 70, 71.)

5. GREAT BLACK-HEADED GULL. Size of Great Black-backed Gull but light grey above. Has black head in breeding plumage, with conspicuous white marks above and below eye, as with Mediterranean Gull. In winter the head is white with dark patches round the eye and dark freckles on crown and nape. The thick, orange bill with dark, swollen, angled tip is characteristic. Flight-feathers largely white. Adult has black and white tips to white outer primaries, immature has blackish outer primaries and a broad black band on the tail, juvenile is mottled dark brown. (See pages 70, 190.)

SERIES 2

1. CASPIAN PLOVER. Size of Ringed Plover. Breeding male as shown. Female and juvenile similar to winter male (shown) but may be rather more buff on forehead and throat and slightly browner on breast band. (See pages 53, 54, 189.)

2. GREATER SAND PLOVER. (See page 53.)

3. KENTISH PLOVER. (See pages 53, 54.)

4. SOCIABLE PLOVER. About the size of Spur-winged Plover, but slimmer, longer. Summer and winter plumage as shown. Sexes alike. In flight, black and white wings and tail. (See pages 57, 189.)

5. DOTTEREL. (See pages 55, 56.)

SERIES 3

LARKS. 1, 2, 3. (See pages 94–96.)

Plate 1. **Series 1.** 1, 1A. White-eyed Gull, adult, immature. 2, 2A. Hemprich's Gull, adult, immature in flight. 3. Slender-billed Gull. 4. Audouin's Gull. 5. Great Black-headed Gull, adult spring.

Series 2. 1. Caspian Plover, winter, summer. 2. Greater Sand Plover, winter, summer. 3. Kentish Plover, immature, adult male. 4. Sociable Plover, winter, summer. 5. Dotterel, summer, winter.

Series 3. Desert Lark, two races. 2. Short-toed Lark, two races. 3. Lesser Short-toed Lark, two races.

I
2
3
2
4
5
6
10
9
7
8
II
13
14
12
S.V.BENSON. 1967

Family BURHINIDAE

STONE CURLEW *Burhinus oedicnemus*. Length 16 in.

RANGE: Lebanon lies in the centre of this bird's breeding range, but it has been recorded only occasionally in spring and autumn, mostly in southern and western areas.

IDENTIFICATION: The light-brown plumage, spotted and streaked, acts as camouflage as the motionless bird 'freezes' into its sandy or earthy background of semi-desert or stony waste, and the pale, rather thick legs look like dried stalks.

The bird walks or runs with lowered head a stealthy stride and with horizontal body, the large yellow eye fixed on the intruder; or squats with head down to the ground, looking like a stone. In flight, dark wing tips and double white wing-bars catch the eye.

NOTES: A phantom-like wailing, double or treble cry, falling and rising, often repeated in quick succession, sometimes curlew-like.

HABITAT: As above.

Plate 2

1. Spotted Eagle, adult.
2. Long-legged Buzzard in flight, beneath and above, light, rufous phase.
3. Buzzard (race, *vulpinus*, Steppe-Buzzard).
4. Kestrel, male.
5. Hobby.
6. Little Owl.
7. Scops Owl.
8. Red-backed Shrike, male.
9. Woodchat Shrike, male.
10. Masked Shrike, male.
11. Black Redstart, male and female (race *semirufus*).
12. Dunn's Lark.
13. Rock Sparrow.
14. Redstart, male, summer.

CREAM-COLOURED COURSER *Cursorius cursor.*
Length 9 in.

RANGE: The range of the Courser, both in summer and winter, lies rather south of Lebanon, to the east and the west. It breeds commonly in Jordan and in Arabian and Syrian deserts and has been recorded from Anti-Lebanon and the Bekaa, where it was suspected of breeding. There are no very recent records.
IDENTIFICATION: The Courser is a bright, sandy, isabelline-colour above, paler on the face, neck and underparts, with black primaries and under-surface of wings and long, very pale, almost white legs. A black stripe curves from the eye to the nape, with a white stripe over it, and the sharp bill is down-curved. On the ground the bird runs fast or crouches to hide rather than take to its wings. In flight is it quick and vigorous, with distinctive contrasting sandy-cream and black plumage, the pointed, plover-shaped wings being black from the bend to the tip above, and all black beneath.
NOTES: Usually silent, but has a short harsh note.
HABITAT: Sandy and stony deserts, often with scanty vegetation.

PRATINCOLE *Glareola pratincola*. Length 10 in.

BLACK-WINGED PRATINCOLE *Glareola nordmanni*. Length 10 in.

RANGE: The Pratincoles are seldom seen except as occasional migrants along the coast. They breed at most points of the compass from Lebanon and winter in Africa and both are likely to occur on passage, though, *G. normanni* has not been mentioned until eleven were recorded in April 1969 on the shore near Sidon.
IDENTIFICATION: Pratincoles are rather tern-like, having short legs, slender, very deeply forked tails and long, sharp wings, narrow and pointed from the bend to the tip. The Black-winged may be distinguished from the other at close range by blackish-brown wings above with blackish under-surface and less clear contrast between the brown mantle and the blackish primaries above, and by lack of white tip edges to secondaries. The Pratincole is distinguished by chestnut wing-linings instead of black, but the difference is very hard to see except in good light at short range. Both have cream-coloured bibs, with (in summer) a black outline. Both have deeply forked, white-edged black tails with white upper tail-coverts and white underparts merging with pale brown breasts below the bib-line.
NOTES: Pratincoles are noisy with tern-like cries, 'kit, kit, kitti, kitti, kitti'.
HABITAT: Plains, mud-flats, marshes, and near lakes or other water.

1. Pratincole, summer. 2. Black-winged Pratincole, summer.
1A. in flight.

BLACK-HEADED GULL *Larus ridibundus.* Length 14½–15 in.

RANGE: Breeds north of Lebanon right across Europe and Asia and winters further south including the Mediterranean. In Lebanon it is common in winter along the coast and off Beirut. Kumerloeve recorded 300–400, and it has been noted from September to April inclusive.

IDENTIFICATION: Like the following, it shows a dark head in breeding plumage, but the hood of this bird is dark chocolate-brown, not really black, and extends on to the crown, but not down the nape as with the following two species. In all seasons it shows a white band on the leading edge of the wing from tip to bend, and a black fringe formed by black primary-tips.

The wing is rather dark on the underside of the primaries (but not on the whole underside of the wing. Compare with Little Gull).

Immature plumage shows less white on the primaries, and, as with most young gulls, has a black band on the tip of the tail, and may show brown mottling on wing-coverts and mantle.

NOTES: Raucous screams 'craar', 'quip' and others.

HABITAT: The sea and shore, rivers and lakes; but on migration as under 'Range'.

summer winter

Page 70

MEDITERRANEAN (BLACK HEADED) GULL

Larus melanocephalus. Length 15–15½ in.

RANGE: Not very uncommon off the shore in autumn and winter. It breeds north of Lebanon and winters in the Mediterranean and elsewhere.
IDENTIFICATION: Only a very little larger than the other Black-headed Gull, *L. ridibundus*, and like it, shows a black head only in breeding plumage. The adult may always be distinguished, however, by the pure white primaries, and in breeding plumage by blacker hood extending to nape. Immature birds are distinguished from *L. ridibundus* by the lack of the white band along the fore-wing of the latter from the tip to the bend.
NOTES: The Mediterranean Gull has raucous screams similar to the Black-headed Gull's.
HABITAT: On passage, the coast, offshore or on the shingle. Occasionally on inland water.

LITTLE GULL *Larus minutus*. Length 11 in.

Page 70

RANGE: Fairly common here in winter offshore, or occasionally on shore. Breeding further north.
IDENTIFICATION: The adult Little Gull has white primary-tips without any black, and is very small. The wings show very dark on the undersides and the wing-ends are more rounded than with any other gull. It also has a black head in breeding plumage. Immature birds, which are white on the underside of the wings, show in flight a black inverted W across the wings above, which includes the black outer primaries. The young Kittiwake shows a similar pattern with the addition of a black collar across the nape, but it is a considerably larger bird.
NOTES: Sometimes has a quiet cluck or a shrill, double, squeaky scream.
HABITAT: As Mediterranean Gull.

1. Mediterranean Gull, adult, winter. 1A. immature. 1B. adult, summer. 2. Common Gull. (See page 190.) 3. Lesser Black-backed Gull. 4. Herring Gull. 5. Little Gull, immature. 5A. adult, winter, from beneath. 5B. adult, summer. 6. Great Black-backed Gull, immature. 7. Lesser Crested Tern. 8. White-winged Black Tern. (See page 190.) 9. Little Tern. 10. and 10A. Common Tern. 11. Audouin's Gull. (See Plate 1, page 64.) 12. Sandwich Tern. (See page 191.) 13. Gull-billed Tern. (See page 191.) All Terns have less black on the crown in autumn-winter, No. 8 becomes grey and white with black nape. (See page 72.)

LESSER BLACK-BACKED GULL *Larus fuscus*. Length 21 in.

HERRING GULL *Larus argentatus*. Length 22 in.

RANGE: *L. fuscus* breeds far north and winters chiefly south of Lebanon. *L. argentatus* breeds in the north, east and west as far south as the Mediterranean coasts, including, fairly recently, the Lebanese islands off Tripoli. Both birds are seen offshore along the Lebanon coast in all seasons. *L. fuscus* is present in higher numbers on migration than at other times, and in spite of the fact that it breeds far away, it is always more numerous up and down the coast than *L. argentatus*.
IDENTIFICATION: They are much the same size, but *L. argentatus* is grey above, while the other is nearly black. Both have black wing-tips with white 'blaze' marks ('mirrors'), but these are larger on *L. argentatus*. Both have yellow bills with a red spot and yellow legs. The race of *L. argentatus* breeding here is *L.a. michahellis*, belonging to the yellow-legged group. Both have immature plumage of dark mottled brown and white with dark brownish wings and tails.
NOTES: Both call with laughing or yelping cries, low quacking chuckles or wailing. The vocal tone of *L. fuscus* is a little deeper.
HABITATS: Outside the breeding season as above.

GREAT BLACK-BACKED GULL *Larus marinus*. Length 27 in.

RANGE: Has a wide ocean range, chiefly from northern Europe to north-east America, and winters southward to the Mediterranean and to the Black and Caspian Seas. A few are seen offshore here in most seasons, chiefly immature birds in autumn and winter.
IDENTIFICATION: Similar to *L. fuscus* but has pale flesh-pink legs. It is much larger, having a wing-span of almost 6 feet, and has a slower wing-beat. Immature plumage also as *L. fuscus*.
NOTES AND HABITAT: As above, but the barking and yelping cries are much deeper.

AUDOUIN'S GULL *Larus audouinii*. Page 64

Though breeding here at the end of the last century on Nakl Island, it is now very rarely recorded. Restricted to Mediterranean area. Very like Herring Gull, having grey mantle and black outer primaries tipped with white spots. Distinguished from latter by rather smaller size, slightly narrower wings, stout, mainly coral-red bill (looking black except at close range), dark eyes and dark grey to greyish-olive legs. (See other Gulls, page 190.)

COMMON TERN *Sterna hirundo*. Length 14 in.

RANGE: A wide breeding range in the northern hemisphere. At the turn of the century it was breeding in abundance on islands off Tripoli and on the coast, but, sad to relate, it now appears to be only a migrant and straggler passing by. It seems that eggs were collected and some birds shot from time to time.
IDENTIFICATION: A slender, pale-grey and white bird, light and airy on the wing as it scans the water for tiny fish or plunges in head first for a catch. It has a black cap and red bill and legs. The latter are very short, which is noticed when the bird alights. The wings are very long, narrow and pointed and the tail long, slender and very deeply forked.
NOTES: All Terns have shrill screams, some harsh and raucous. The Common Tern has a grating scream, and 'kirri-kirri-kirri', 'kit', etc.
HABITAT: On migration as above. In other countries many are seen on inland waters as well as on the sea shore and islands, and breed colonially on shingle or dunes.

LITTLE TERN *Sterna albifrons*. Length 9½ in. Page 70

RANGE: A wide breeding range, as Common Tern, and formerly breeding with it on the islands off Tripoli. Now only a passing migrant and casual visitor.
IDENTIFICATION: The Little Tern is quite small, looking half the size of the above, with faster wing-beats and more hovering. It appears all whitish, but is very pale grey above. It has an incomplete black cap with a broad white forehead-band reaching to the eye. (Do not confuse with Terns of other species with white foreheads in autumn and winter.) The bill and legs are yellow, the former with a black tip.
NOTES: Has similar cries to Common Tern and a double, rasping 'cree-ik', also similar habitat.

LESSER CRESTED TERN *Sterna bengalensis*. Page 70

Bred here on Nakl Island at the end of the last century. No recent records. Breeds on North African coast, Red Sea eastward and southward. A large Tern similar to the Sandwich and Gull-billed Terns, but with an all yellow bill and grey, forked tail. (See page 191.)

Family COLUMBIDAE

ROCK DOVE *Columba livia*. Length 13 in.

RANGE: Lebanon lies in the centre of the wide breeding range of this species in Europe, Asia and Africa. Some birds are resident in the mountains of Lebanon and Anti-Lebanon in steep ravines, river-side cliffs, caverns and rocks at considerable altitudes where they appear to be breeding.
IDENTIFICATION: The Rock Dove is well known in its domestic and sporting forms as racing pigeons and some types of town pigeons. It is grey with a double black wing-bar, whitish rump, and irridescent purple and green on the neck.
NOTES: A low cooing as with domestic birds.
HABITAT: As above.

1. Rock Dove. 2. Turtle Dove. 3. Palm Dove.

TURTLE DOVE *Streptopelia turtur*. Length 11 in.

RANGE: The bulk of the Turtle Dove's breeding range lies north and east of Lebanon, but it breeds in Cyprus and Syria and also in parts of Africa, and it is local in Lebanon. It is an abundant passage migrant to and from more northerly breeding areas and thousands of more than one race and shade are shot and offered for sale. I have seen bunches amounting to fifty or sixty at a time, mostly of the European or northern race.
IDENTIFICATION: A sandy red-brown mantle with blackish spots, dark wing-tips and blackish tail with white border and sides. The tail is round-ended, and when it is fanned before alighting the white border catches the eye. The head and part of the wing-coverts are blue-grey, the throat and upper breast lavender-pinkish and the underparts whitish. There is a patch on each side of the neck of fine black and white stripes. The local form is paler and has less chestnut on the mantle and fainter spots.
NOTES: A soft purring coo in breeding area.
HABITAT: Open country with trees, plantations, groves or bushes.

PALM DOVE or LAUGHING DOVE Page 73
Streptopelia senegalensis. Length $10\frac{1}{4}$ in.

RANGE: A familiar resident in Beirut where it breeds in the American University campus and also in the town centre where it is seen among the palm trees. It has also been recorded in gardens in Chtoura in the Bekaa. The breeding range is from Africa to south-east Turkey and eastward through Asia.
IDENTIFICATION: The Palm Dove is rather smaller than the Turtle Dove with shorter wings and proportionately longer, slightly pointed tail. It is rather sandy or copper-brown above, paler beneath with a collar in front of rust with blackish spots; cinnamon or pink-tinted on head and breast, blue-grey on wing-coverts and greyish on rump. The tail is dark with white sides and tips of outer feathers, as with Turtle Dove.
NOTES: Loud, harsh cries and a rising and falling staccato cooing or chuckling note, from which it gets its name of Laughing Dove.
HABITAT: Under 'Range'.

Family CUCULIDAE

CUCKOO *Cuculus canorus*. Length 13 in.

RANGE: The Cuckoo has a great breeding range in Europe, Asia and Africa, and winters in Africa. In Lebanon it breeds in the mountains where and when unmolested by shooters.
IDENTIFICATION: Blue-grey above, including head and throat, with white underparts heavily barred with dark grey, and a long graduated tail spotted and tipped white. Juveniles and, more rarely, females may be rufous and barred all over. Other immature birds are grey-brown and barred. They have a narrow whitish patch on the nape. The barred, chestnut, Kestrel-colouring in females may be fairly common here. I have seen two, including a bird shot near the northern border with Syria, and Tristram described a reddish variety he called '*Cuculus libanoticus*' in the last century.
NOTES: Besides the well known 'cook-coo', there is a harsh, low note and the female makes a long bubbling sound.
HABITAT: Open country with some trees or bushes, usually in the hills. Occasionally in groves and gardens by the coast on passage. It lays its eggs, singly, in the nests of small birds, often those of Larks and Pipits.

GREAT SPOTTED CUCKOO *Clamator glandarius*. Length $15\frac{1}{2}$ in.

RANGE: The Great Spotted Cuckoo has a much more restricted breeding range than the Cuckoo, chiefly in isolated areas in some Mediterranean countries, and the Levant and Turkey eastward. In Lebanon it breeds in the mountains, perhaps very thinly. I have seen it in mid-May near Ainata and in north Lebanon and there are other spring records within the breeding season. It is also a migrant on passage in late February, March and April and again in late summer and autumn.

IDENTIFICATION: Dark greyish-brown above with white flecks. The dark tail is more graduated and longer than the Cuckoo's and shows white at the sides and tip. The underparts are creamy white and there is a conspicuous crest on the head. The immature bird has no crest and has chestnut primaries.

NOTES: A harsh chatter and other deep harsh single calls.

HABITAT: As Cuckoo. It lays its eggs, several together, in the nests of Crows and probably Jays in Lebanon.

SCOPS OWL *Otus scops*. Length $7\frac{1}{2}$ in.

RANGE: The breeding range includes north-west Africa, southern Europe and the Levant eastward across Asia, and there are other races in mid and South Africa. In Lebanon it is not uncommon where trees of any kind will give it shelter, and appears to breed from the valleys to about 5,000 feet.
IDENTIFICATION: A tiny Owl with beautifully patterned (vermiculated, spotted, barred and streaked) brown plumage and a chain of large whitish spots crossing the scapulars. It is one of the smallest owls with ear-tufts. Eyes bright yellow. The ground-colour of the plumage varies considerably from the very grey-brown races of the Levant to the more rufous or sandy brown of a more western and northern race which has been seen here on passage.
NOTES: A pretty, plaintive whistle, generally repeated every few seconds for considerable periods from a hidden perch.
HABITAT: Strictly nocturnal, in trees, plantations, and ruins. In countries where it is unmolested, it is more often found in town trees and avenues.

LITTLE OWL *Athene noctua*. Length $8\frac{1}{2}$ in. Page 65

RANGE: Lebanon is in the wide breeding range of the Little Owl which lies right across Europe, Asia and North Africa.
IDENTIFICATION: Not so small and distinctly stouter and more squat than the Scops, with a flat head and no 'ears'. It is brown, spotted and barred with white above and whitish beneath streaked with brown, and has bright yellow eyes.
NOTES: A high, plaintive whistle and a barking note, mewing and snoring.
HABITAT: Open country, dry mountains, rocks, trees, buildings, etc. It may be seen perched in the open in daylight. In other countries it is found more in gardens and towns than it is here.

BROWN FISH-OWL *Ketupa zeylonensis*.

One specimen in A.U.B. museum, Beirut. Breeds in parts of the Levant, including Jordan, south-eastward through Asia. A large, bulky-looking, streaky brown owl with 'ear'-tufts. The call is 'a deep, hollow, moaning "boom-o-boom" uttered at sundown on leaving the day-time retreat, and during the night and early morning' (Salim Ali).

TAWNY OWL *Strix aluco*. Length 15 in.

RANGE: Lebanon lies on the southern limit of the Tawny Owl's breeding range. It appears that both this and the Barn Owl are seen occasionally at various times of the year and may have maintained a precarious hold in some quieter valleys and other places where trees offer protection.
IDENTIFICATION: A plump, rounded brown owl of variable shade, greyer or more reddish in colour, paler beneath with dark, barbed streaks, and with large creamy spots and thin dark streaks above. The facial disc is lighter with large dark eyes.
NOTES: A long, musical, eerie, wavering 'hoo-hoo-oo-oooooo', and a sharp 'tu-wick'.
HABITAT: Chiefly in woods, also gardens and trees. Perches out of sight in daylight. (See other owls on pages 12 and 13.)

BARN OWL *Tyto alba*. Length $13\frac{1}{2}$ in.

RANGE: An almost worldwide range including most of Europe, Africa and southern Asia. In Lebanon both this and the Tawny are rather scarce, lacking both the habitat and the protection needful for successful residence and breeding in most areas. Many are shot but it is to be hoped that others are overlooked rather than wiped out.
IDENTIFICATION: It is a slimmer, more upright bird than the Tawny when perched. Plumage variable, but a white-breasted race is usual in the Lebanon area. The upper parts are sandy-buff speckled with light grey, and the bird looks whitish on the wing and occasionally appears in daylight, when it shows soft, rounded wings, as other owls, and the white face and underparts. The legs and toes are also feathered in white.
NOTES: A tearing, rending sound or split-screech, also hisses, snores and has a sharp yapping note.
HABITAT: Gorges, cliffs, rocks, ruins, barns, woods, gardens, and sometimes desert.

Family CAPRIMULGIDAE

NIGHTJAR *Caprimulgus europaeus*. Length 10½ in.

RANGE: Lebanon apparently lies on the southern limit of the breeding range, and nesting seems rare, but the bird is not uncommon on passage in spring and autumn.
IDENTIFICATION: With flitting, silent flight, hawk-like silhouette and crepuscular and nocturnal habits, the Nightjar is an interesting bird. On migration it is seen more frequently in daylight. At other times it usually lies up by day, its brown and grey dead-leaf or bark-patterned plumage being wonderful camouflage as it crouches on the ground, among stones, or scrub. When perched on a tree it usually takes up its position crouching along the branch rather than crossing it. At dusk it catches flying insects, usually moths and beetles which fly in the evening. It has long wings and tail and a flat, swift-like head with similar large gape and small bill. The male has a blotch of white near the wing-tip and white on the tips of the outer tail-feathers. Both sexes are barred, mottled and vermiculated with grey, brown, black and buff.
NOTES: 'coo-ik', and a sharp 'quik, quik, quik'. The song at dusk or darkness is a soft purring trill, generally rising and falling or fading and strengthening, usually continuous for minutes at a time.
HABITAT: As above.

Plate 3

1. Bee-eater. 2. Blue-cheeked Bee-eater. 3. Roller.

1
2
1
2
3
S.V. Benson

1
2
3
4
5
6
7
8
7A
7A
9
10
11
12
13

LITTLE SWIFT or HOUSE SWIFT *Apus affinis*. Length about 5 in.

RANGE: This bird used to be called White-rumped Swift, though there are other Swifts with white rumps in Africa and the Far East. It ranges from Africa through Arabia, Jordan, Palestine and Syria eastward through south Asia, and has been recorded a number of times in Lebanon river valleys in spring in flocks or small parties. However, some doubt seems to have arisen about the records of breeding in Lebanon, though eggs were collected.
IDENTIFICATION: Blackish above and below with brown wings and a white rump, chin and throat, and a whitish forehead merging into pale brownish crown. It is much smaller than the other Swifts of the Levant. Seen in flight from beneath, in sunshine, it may appear to be a white-headed swift with an almost square-ended tail. From above it may be confused with the House Martin, though the light brown head and brown wings and tail distinguish it as well as the narrow, longer shape of the wings which is typical of Swifts.
NOTES: A thin, shrill, trilling scream, less powerful than those of other Swifts. The birds are gregarious, chasing each other in aerial play, screaming or chittering as they sweep to and fro.
HABITAT: Cliffs, gorges, ravines and caverns. Nesting-colonies in caverns and cliffs or on buildings.

PALLID SWIFT *Apus pallidus*. Length 6½ in. Page 82

RANGE: Chiefly a Mediterranean breeding area, extending to parts of south-east Asia. Winters in Africa. Few records here. Some over Tripoli May 1956 (Hollom).
IDENTIFICATION: Looks like a pale version of the common Swift, being grey-brown instead of blackish, and having paler wing-linings than the flight feathers, while the common Swift has the reverse. It also has a much larger area of whitish on the throat. Notes are as common Swift.
HABITAT: Cliffs, caverns, ravines, gorges, towns and villages.

Plate 4
1. Wall Creeper, summer.
2. House Martin.
3. Little Swift.
4. Red-rumped Swallow.
5. Golden Oriole, adult male.
6. Pied Kingfisher.
7. Smyrna Kingfisher, with 7A spread wing.
8. Red-breasted Flycatcher, adult male.
9. Goldcrest.
10. Lesser Whitethroat.
11. Sardinian Warbler.
12. Rufous Bush Robin.
13. Kingfisher.

1. Pallid Swift. 2. Swift. 3. Alpine Swift.
4. Swallow. 5. Red-rumped Swallow.

SWIFT *Apus apus*. Length 6½ in.

RANGE: Breeds in Europe and Asia and in parts of extreme North Africa. Winters in Africa. Though a summer visitor to Lebanon, breeding where possible, the great majority of the large numbers seen in spring and autumn are on migration.
IDENTIFICATION: Usually seen in flight with others. Looks larger and is longer-winged than Martins and Swallows. Sooty blackish all over except for whitish chin which is difficult to detect. The narrow curved wings are scythe-shaped and are moved very rapidly between intervals of gliding. In breeding areas usually three or more birds are seen skimming around chasing each other with high, shrill screaming.
NOTES: Usually a very high, metallic, piercing scream when on the wing.
HABITAT: It lives mostly on the wing, hawking for insects, but will cling to a cliff or the wall of a building. It nests in crevices in cliffs or mountain crags and also in tall buildings, and, especially in northern Europe and Asia, in holes in trees.

ALPINE SWIFT *Apus melba*. Length 8¼ in.

RANGE: Breeds in south Europe, west Asia and the Medtierranean area, including a few places in the Lebanon mountains, also in South and East Africa, and winters in the southern part of its range.
IDENTIFICATION: A very large and handsome Swift, having grey-brown plumage with white underparts divided from the white throat by a broad dark-brown band across the upper breast.
NOTES: A high chattering, trilling cry as it skims to and fro usually with others. The note is more of a trill than the Swift's and swells and dies away as the birds dash round and round.
HABITAT: High rocky mountains, ravines, cliffs and crags, also old viaducts and sometimes ruined buildings for nesting crevices.

ROLLER *Coracias garrulus*. Length 12 in.

RANGE: Breeds in southern and eastern Europe and in parts of Asia, also in extreme north-west Africa; winters in Africa and India. In the Lebanon it is an abundant migrant in spring and autumn. Though said to breed successfully as far south as the highlands of Palestine, in Syria and certainly in Cyprus, it has little inducement to do so in Lebanon, not only because of the very large numbers which are shot in the hills in spring, but because of the lack of suitable trees and other nesting-sites.

IDENTIFICATION: This is one of the most beautiful, perhaps the most colourful bird seen in Lebanon. The plumage is vivid light blue with a bright chestnut-tawny mantle and deep violet or purple-blue shoulders to the wings. The lower back and rump are also violet. The light-blue wings are heavily fringed with near-black: a striking feature when the bird is in flight. The blue tail has a greenish-brown centre and black tips to the two outer feathers. It is large for so brightly-coloured a bird, and is but little smaller than a Jay or Jackdaw. The flight is usually light and strong, and in display the bird will roll and tumble about on the wing, sometimes hurtling down from a considerable height and flopping from side to side.

NOTES: A harsh, loud chatter or deep 'kr-r-ark'.

HABITAT: On migration it may turn up anywhere, but is chiefly seen in the hills. It seeks old, hollow trees and ruins for nesting-holes, and sometimes crevices in cliffs or crags, and frequents parks and open country. It feeds largely on grasshoppers, locusts and other large insects and centipedes and lizards, and is most beneficial to agriculture.

PIED KINGFISHER *Ceryle rudis*. Length 10–11 in.

RANGE: The breeding area is in Africa and the Levant eastward, including Jordan. In Lebanon it is mainly an autumn and winter visitor to the coast, estuaries and rivers.
IDENTIFICATION: Unmistakable with its black and white plumage and crested head, especially when it is fluttering with rounded black and white wings over water, or plunging in with large dagger-like bill aimed at a fish. The back is barred and blotched with black and white, the underparts white. The male has a double black bib-border, the female an incomplete single one, immature birds have just a smudge.
NOTES: A shrill, vibrant or whinneying whistle.

SMYRNA KINGFISHER *Halcyon smyrnensis*. Length about 11½ in.

Page 81

RANGE: The Smyrna or White-breasted Kingfisher's breeding area is from the Levant, including Jordan, eastward in southern Asia. In Lebanon it has been recorded in autumn, winter and early spring at Ammiq Swamp and also by the rivers.
IDENTIFICATION: Pale aquamarine and bright turquoise blue (looking royal blue at some angles) on the back, wings and tail, with white on the throat and centre of the breast, and dark chestnut-red on the head, 'shoulders', sides of the breast and the rest of the underparts. Legs and massive bill deep red.
NOTES: A strange, laughing call, sometimes loud and rattling, or recalling the Green Woodpecker's yaffle, sometimes subdued. There is also a trill which is probably the song. 'A noisy bird with raucous stropping or pumping call "chuk-chuk-chukkeruk" etc.' . . . also 'a high-pitched rapid, descending call, like a giant Babbler'—April-May. (Moor and Boswell.) 'May-June, one used to give display flights from the date gardens in the early mornings . . . lolloping up to about 150–200 feet, screaming loudly. . . . Then come down in a steep, fairly tight spiral.' (Williamson.) 'A loud rattling "chake, ake, ake-ake-ake-ake"' . . . also 'tittering (song?) on a descending scale "ti-ti-ti-ti-ti-ti-ti-ti-tieu" of which the first two-thirds sounded at a distance like a Whimbrel.' (Hollom.)

KINGFISHER *Alcedo atthis*. Length 6½ in.

RANGE: A great breeding range across Europe, Asia and a large part of Africa. Here it is seen in all seasons and doubtless still tries to breed up the mountain streams and rivers, when circumstances permit. It is chiefly seen, however, along the coast in autumn and winter, also sometimes in spring in estuaries, rivers, by any inland water and frequently at Ammiq Swamp.
IDENTIFICATION: The Kingfisher is brilliant blue above, greener on the wings and scapulars, and orange-chestnut beneath with white patches on the sides of the neck and chin. It is a very small bird with a big head and dagger bill and may be seen flying on a bee-line with rapid wings moving so fast as to escape the eye and appear blurred, or it may be seen hovering over the water or plunging like other Kingfishers.
NOTES: A very shrill, high, trilling whistle.
HABITAT: As above.

BEE-EATER *Merops apiaster*. Length 11 in.

PERSIAN or BLUE-CHEEKED BEE-EATER
Merops superciliosus. Length about 12 in.

RANGE: The main breeding range of the Bee-eater is in southern Europe eastward to mid-Asia, including the Mediterranean area. *M. superciliosus* breeds in parts of North and East Africa and the Levant eastward to parts of western and southern Asia. Neither has been as successful in breeding here as could be wished, presumably because of what Kumerloeve* calls 'the permanent killing by hunters or "sportsmen".' A small colony of *M. superciliosus* was recorded breeding near Beirut in 1945, otherwise it appears to be almost unknown in Lebanon. *M. apiaster*, however, is a common migrant in fair numbers every spring and autumn, usually to be heard and seen in small flocks from sea level to 6,000 feet.

IDENTIFICATION: *M. apiaster* is a delicately shaped and gorgeously coloured bird with a thin, sharp, slightly down-curved bill. The upperparts are coppery-chestnut and yellow, the wings and tail blue-green, the underparts bright turquoise-blue, the throat buttercup-yellow with a thin black band dividing it from the green-blue underparts. The central tail feathers are long and narrowly pointed. *M. superciliosus* is green both above and below with a little blue on the forehead, on the supercilium (eyebrow-streak) and on the cheeks, and black on the ear-coverts. The chin and throat are yellow and chestnut without the outline to the throat-panel. In shape and size it is like *M. apiaster*, but longer points to central tail feathers give a longer measurement.

NOTES: *M. apiaster*, 'Prook, prook', usually in chorus, or 'quilp, quilp'. *M. superciliosus* has a harsher, lower note, also in chorus, said to be more vibrant and disyllabic.

HABITAT: Bushy or scrubby hills, tops of ravines, trees, telegraph wires, even Beirut TV masts. On migration, flocks glide high overhead calling constantly.

* *Notes on the Birds of the Lebanese Republic* by H. Kumerloeve.

Family UPUPIDAE

HOOPOE *Upupa epops*. Length 11 in.

RANGE: The breeding range is right across the warmer parts of Europe and Asia, and in most parts of Africa. In Lebanon it is a common migrant in spring and autumn to all areas, especially near the coast, and in the shelter of gardens.

Ceaseless persecution, however, prevents settling in and breeding though there are also a few summer and winter records. The majority winter in Africa and southern Asia.

IDENTIFICATION: Cinnamon or pale pinkish-brown plumage with wings, back and tail strikingly barred with wide bands of black and white; also a black-tipped cockatoo-like crest, raised briefly on alighting or when excited, and a long, slender down-curving bill. Flight shows rounded moth like-wings, often with airy, leisurely wing beats.

NOTES: Sometimes a low chatter or mewing. Usual note or song a hollow, rather soft, 'Hoop, hoop, hoop, hoop'.

HABITAT: Orchards, vines, agricultural plantations, gardens and open, bushy or tree-sprinkled country, broken ground, rocks, walls.

WRYNECK *Jynx torquilla*. Length 6½ in.

RANGE: This is a migrant breeding north of Lebanon right across Europe and central Asia and wintering in Africa. In Lebanon, in spring and autumn, a sprinkle of single Wrynecks appear anywhere along the coastal strip, in river valleys, along the plain of Bekaa or in the outskirts of Beirut.
IDENTIFICATION: The plumage above is brown and grey with buff and black spots and other markings, paler beneath with dense barring. The back has a tree-bark pattern; the tail is more broadly barred and the wings checkered. As with other Woodpeckers the feet have two toes forward and two back. On the ground it hops about and looks something like a long, heavy sparrow from a distance. At close range, when clinging to a wall or tree it may look reptilian with snake-skin patterns on the back and the head facing the tail, an attitude which earned it its English name. The crown feathers can be raised in a bushy crest.
NOTES: A loud, peevish, often persistent "pew, pew, pew, pew'.
HABITAT: Trees, orchards, vines, agriculture, thickets, walls.

SYRIAN WOODPECKER *Dendrocopus syriacus*. Length 9 in.

RANGE: The Syrian Woodpecker is resident from Turkey and the Levant eastward beyond the Persian Gulf in south-east Iran, and also in parts of south-east Europe, but here, though probably still resident in north Lebanon, it has very rarely been recorded in recent years.

IDENTIFICATION: It resembles the Great Spotted Woodpecker, but the cheek and side of the neck show an uninterrupted white area without the black bar which crosses the cheek to the nape in the latter, and it has no more than a black, curving band from the bill to the side of the upper breast. As with the Great Spotted, the back, wings and tail are black, the wings barred with white and with a large white patch on the scapulars. Crown black, nape red, underparts creamy-whitish, under the tail red. Immature birds, as with Great Spotted, have red caps.

NOTES: A sharp 'quick, quick'.

HABITAT: Trees of all kinds and often cultivation.

SAND MARTIN *Riparia riparia*. Length 4¾ in.

RANGE: Worldwide through Europe, Asia and North America. It is a common autumn migrant and a scarcer early spring one, on passage to and from Africa. Breeding is not recorded here though many have been seen in twos and threes in May near the coast, up river valleys and on the mountains.
IDENTIFICATION: Both these Martins have forked tails, but neither has the deep fork and long outer feathers of the Swallow's tail. The Sand Martin is grey-brown on the whole upper side and the white underparts are crossed by a brown band on the upper breast.
NOTES: Twitters on the wing.
HABITAT: River valleys or near any water, plains, and the coast. Gregarious, almost always on the wing hawking insects. For the nesting hole it makes a tunnel in a sandy cliff or river bank in a colony with others.

HOUSE MARTIN *Delichon urbica*. Length 5 in. Pages 81, 92

RANGE: Very widespread in Europe and Asia, from which it migrates to Africa. Lebanon lies towards the southern limit of its breeding range. Seen on passage near the coast in moderate numbers in spring and autumn, and all over Lebanon in spring. A few breed in towns where permitted, and many breed in the gorge below the Cedars and probably elsewhere in sheltered ravines.
IDENTIFICATION: Rather easily recognized with black above except for the conspicuous white rump, and white beneath.
NOTES: Twitters on the wing. The scolding cry is a very shrill 't-seep'.
HABITAT: As Sand Martin, gregarious, nearly always on the wing, or sometimes congregates on telephone wires, roof ridges or clings to the face of a cliff. Builds a globular mud nest with an entrance hole near the upper edge under a rock-ledge or under the eaves of a building.

CRAG MARTIN *Hirundo rupestris*. Length 5¾ in.

RANGE: Breeds in southern Europe and Mediterranean area including the Levant, southward in parts of Africa and eastward right through parts of south and mid-Asia. Here it breeds in the mountains from a few hundred to nearly 9,000 feet in Lebanon and Anti-Lebanon, but nowhere in more than very small groups. In winter, it may sometimes be seen at lower levels.
IDENTIFICATION: It resembles the Sand Martin in colour, but it is a larger, less slender bird with square-cut tail, brownish-white underparts, no breast-band and a few white spots in the tail which do not catch the eye except at close quarters when the tail is spread.
NOTES: An occasional small squeaky note.
HABITAT: Mountain cliffs, gorges and steep rocks. The nest is built of mud, like a half-cup stuck to the face of a rock, generally under an over-hang or mountain road-bridge or in a cave.

1. Sand Martin. 2. House Martin. 3. Crag Martin.

Page 82

SWALLOW *Hirundo rustica*. Length $7\frac{1}{2}$ in.

RANGE: The breeding range is worldwide in Europe, Asia and North America, including all countries bordering the Mediterranean. In Lebanon it is a common and abundant migrant in spring and autumn. The race breeding to the north with a white to pale pinkish-buff breast passes through. The race breeding from Lebanon to Palestine, *H.r. transitiva*, has variable reddish-buff underparts, but not so dark as the dark reddish underparts of the Egyptian race.
IDENTIFICATION: Distinguished from the Martins by its long, thin outer tail feathers and deeply forked tail. It is steel-blue (often appearing blue-black) above and white to reddish-buff beneath, with brick-red forehead and throat bordered on the lower throat by a band of dark blue. White marks in the tail may be seen at close quarters.
NOTES: Twittering. The twittering song ends with a dry scraping note, and the alarm is shrill and metallic. The flight-note is a sharp 'tweet'.
HABITAT: Often seen skimming over water or hawking insects in any part of the country. It builds an open part-mud nest on a ledge or beam in a building.

RED-RUMPED SWALLOW *Hirundo daurica*. Length 7 in.

Pages 81, 82

RANGE: In parts of southern Europe, mid to south Asia and in Africa. Here it is not a very common migrant, breeding in some of the river valleys near the coast, sometimes abundant in Litani river valley in spring, probably wintering in Africa.
IDENTIFICATION: Distinguished by pinkish-buff rump and underparts without a dark bib, a reddish-buff collar, and by shorter streamers than the Swallow's to the deeply forked tail. The rump can look nearly white at a distance.
NOTES: Twittering and a deeper, musical note. Flight-note hoarse and thin.
HABITAT: Ravines and low land, rivers and other water. The nest is bottle-shaped with spout-shaped entrance, on the underside of the overhang of a rock, bridge or building.

DUNN'S LARK *Eremalauda dunni*. Length about $5\frac{1}{2}$ in.

There has been at least one certain record of this species in Lebanon and it is not uncommon in a few localities in Jordan where it breeds. It is very similar to the Bar-tailed Desert Lark *Ammomanes cincturus* (see page 206) except for the streaked crown and stouter yellowish-horn bill; smaller than Desert Lark, with pale sandy to pinkish isabelline upperparts faintly mottled with deeper sandy markings, and streaked on the crown and nape to upper mantle with fine brown striations which are darker in this race (*E.d. eremodites*) from Arabia and Jordan than in African birds. The pale pinkish-isabelline wings are tipped with dark brown as with *A. cincturus*, but most of the tail-feathers instead of being only tipped dark, as with *cincturus*, are blackish with narrow russet edgings, the outer pair edged buff. The tapering, pointed central tail-feathers are bright sandy-colour. The whitish underparts are tinted on the flanks and upper breast with sandy-buff and faintly spotted with pale brown on the upper breast. Small dark spots form a moustachial streak on each side of the white throat. Legs pale biscuit.

DESERT LARK *Ammomanes deserti*. Length $5\frac{3}{4}$–6 in.
Pages 64, 100

Breeds in Syria southward and eastward and in Africa, and is common in parts of Jordan. A few have been recorded in Lebanon in autumn. A mediumly small lark with yellowish bill. The Syrian desert race is pale sandy or pinkish isabelline. The Jordan valley birds are pale brown with faint breast-spotting and a rusty tone in part of the wing and on the rump. Birds of the black lava deserts are dusky. Has soft, high call note and sweet 'tee-too-wee' repeated in descending, gliding song-flight, or sung from a rock or the ground, sometimes followed by low 'chirra-ra'.

BIFASCIATED or HOOPOE LARK *Alaemon alaudipes*.
Length $7\frac{1}{2}$ in. Page 100

Breeds south and east of Lebanon, including Jordan. It is very large, tall and slender, with very pale sandy or pale grey-brown plumage with blackish spots on the upper breast, pale eyebrow stripe, dark stripe through eye, longish tail and down-curved bill. It runs with long whitish legs, but when flushed shows striking bands of blackish and white along the wings. A few have been shot in the Bekaa in autumn.

SHORT-TOED LARK *Calandrella cinerea*. Length $5\frac{1}{2}$ in.

RANGE: Southern Europe eastward through Asia, and parts of Africa. Here it seems to be breeding not only in Anti-Lebanon but on the east side of the Lebanon range and in the Bekaa in very small numbers. Both this and the Lesser Short-toed Lark are seen, sometimes in large numbers, on passage in autumn. Some flocks appear along the coastal strip, but most of the great autumn movements are in the Bekaa, flying and feeding with migrating Calandras.

IDENTIFICATION: Small, without a crest and with a short, pale, yellowish bill. Creamy-white underparts are without spots or streaks sometimes showing a small dark or blackish mark on each side of the throat. The upperparts are streaked light brown with near white on some outer tail-feathers. Most tail-feathers are very dark with pale edges. From beneath, the flying and singing bird shows a small blackish tail with whitish edging. Occasionally the crown may have a warmer buff or reddish shade, and in other geographical variations the plumage may be sandy, reddish or of a colder grey or grey-brown.

NOTES: The call note is a soft 'chup' or chirrup described as sparrow-like. The song is a high-pitched twittering as the bird rises and falls like a yo-yo in the air, often with long spells of singing. B. W. Tucker mentions a plaintive note, 'tee-oo' and gives the song as 'tee-tsit-wee, tsi-wichoo' repeated again and again.

HABITAT: Chiefly open places, plains and grassland.

LESSER SHORT-TOED LARK *Calandrella rufescens*. Lenght $5\frac{1}{4}$–$5\frac{1}{2}$ in.

RANGE: Right across central Asia, also in North Africa and southern Spain. Here it is chiefly a migrant. (See Short-toed Lark.)
IDENTIFICATION: Distinguished from Short-toed Lark by fine streaks on the breast and face (visible at close range) as well as on the upperparts which vary in shade in different parts of the range from pale reddish-brown to light grey-brown (darker and greyer in Spanish race with heavier breast streaks). But the two species are best distinguished from one another by the call notes.
NOTES: 'prrrt', a harsher rattle than that of Short-toed, and a sweet little song when rising in circling song-flight.
HABITAT: Arid semi-deserts and salt flats.

Bimaculated Lark (a song-stance). It also sings while walking and running. (See opposite.)

CALANDRA LARK *Melanocorypha calandra*. Length $7\frac{1}{2}$ in.

BIMACULATED LARK or EASTERN CALANDRA *Melanocorypha bimaculata*. Length $6\frac{1}{2}$ in.

RANGE: The breeding area of the Calandra is all around the Mediterranean, north and eastward to central Asia, that of the Bimaculated is in western Asia including the Levant. In Lebanon both breed, the Calandra in the Bekaa (when surviving) and on the lower slopes of Anti-Lebanon and the Bimaculated in the high mountains of Lebanon and Hermon areas, where it was once abundant, but is so no more. The Calandra prefers cultivated areas. Both are migrants and winter visitors and great flocks of mixed larks pass through the Bekaa in autumn moving further south.
IDENTIFICATION: Large, heavy, short-tailed Larks without a crest and with a stout almost Bunting-type palish or yellowish bill and a black necklace, usually interrupted in the centre or showing as a dark smudgy bar, widest and blackest on each side of the lower throat. Young birds may show only an indistinct dark patch each side. The Calandra in flight shows large, wide-based wings which look very dark from beneath, with a contrasting whitish rear fringe and a dark tail with white on outer tail feathers. It tends to have a thick, clear, single black bar or patch on each side of the lower throat, usually not quite meeting in the centre. The Bimaculated is smaller and more reddish-sandy, lacking the white on the outer tail feathers and on the tips of the secondaries and inner primaries, which is a feature of the Calandra. But the Bimaculated has white spots on the tips of the tail-feathers which show as a narrow whitish border to the tip of the spread tail in flight. It has a wide, pale superciliary-stripe and darker crown, plainer sandy nape, back of neck and rump, and streaked back. It also tends to a more variable necklace-line. This may be double, may join in the centre or be mottled in the centre and double at the sides. Most often it is formed by two black crescents meeting on the throat. (See opposite.)
NOTES: Flight notes of both are like those of other larks, but often harsher. Songs loud and varied, sometimes like Sky Lark's. Bimaculated often recalls twitters of the Short-toed, interspersed with a churring twitter or rattle. Both sing from the ground as well as on the wing.
HABITAT: Above.

BLACK LARK *Melanocorypha yeltoniensis.*

One autumn record. Range north and east of Lebanon. Calandra-size, with similar stout yellowish bill. No white feathers in wing or tail. Male black in summer, but after autumn moult it is covered with scale-like pale or whitish markings which almost hide the black on upperparts. Winter female and juvenile are very like Calandra, but paler, often more spotted and scaly-looking, until summer, when female is darker brown above and may become variably dusky beneath. In flight she shows very dark brown axillaries and under wing-coverts forming a large dark patch under the wing.

HORNED LARK or SHORE LARK *Eremophila alpestris.*

Length $6\frac{1}{2}$ in. Page 100

RANGE: Includes extreme northern Europe and Asia, North America, North Africa, and some eastern Mediterranean countries eastward through central Asia also. In Lebanon the race *E.a. bicornis* is resident and breeding in the highest parts of Lebanon and Anti-Lebanon ranges, wintering at lower levels, feeding in flocks in autumn.

IDENTIFICATION: It is pinkish grey-brown above with whitish forehead, throat and underparts. Above the forehead is a black band and two little black whisps or 'horns'. Black cheek-patches curve down the sides of the neck to the black bib, usually joining it, in this race, but I have also seen at 5,000–6,000 feet on the Lebanon range in May single birds in which the black cheek-patch was separate from the bib. The tail shows white on outer feathers. Females show rather less black and young birds distinctly less with brown mottlings.

NOTES: A high, shrill flight-note, sometimes pipit-like. The song is a rather feeble, sweet little warbling from the ground, from a stone or on the wing.

HABITAT: High mountain regions above the tree line or with junipers. In winter it descends to hills and plains, sometimes to the Bekaa. In other countries it winters along the sea shore.

CRESTED LARK *Galerida cristata.* Length 6¾ in.

RANGE: The breeding range is widespread through Europe, Asia and Africa. In Lebanon it is resident and breeding, but never in large numbers owing to incessant shooting. The local race is *G.c. cinnamomina*, a sandy, reddish-tinted, or cinnamon variety. In autumn, flocks which are not of the sandy race, form in the high mountains at 6,000–8,000 feet. They are very grey in appearance with almost black-centred tails with bright orange outer tail-feathers, and are indistinguishable from Thekla Larks. The colour of Crested Larks varies to a striking degree according to local habitat, as may be seen in the birds of these local winter movements or partial migrations.
IDENTIFICATION: A medium to large Lark with sandy, warm-brown, streaked plumage, pale beneath with streaks on the breast, and with a tall pointed crest on the head. The tail is very dark in the centre with orange-buff on the outer features.
NOTES: A plaintive, sweet 'pee-weoo' or 'pee-wee-tooi'. The song is shorter than the Sky Lark's with some plaintive notes included. Singing may be from the ground, the top of a boulder, or on the wing.
HABITAT: Hills of the coastal strip and sometimes plains with some cultivation. Very thinly distributed chiefly in areas of sandy soil at about 3,000 feet or less, on the western slopes. Autumn flocks from other localities or races at 6,000 feet upward in the high mountains.

1. Desert Lark. 2 and 2A. Hoopoe Lark. 3. Short-toed Lark. 4. Lesser Short-toed Lark. 5. Calandra Lark. 5A. Bimaculated Lark. 6 and 6A. Horned Lark. 7. Crested Lark. 8. Wood Lark. 9. Sky Lark.

WOOD LARK *Lullula arborea.* Length 6 in.

RANGE: The breeding range is in Europe and west Asia, also in the mountains of part of North Africa. In Lebanon it is resident in moderately small numbers, breeding in the mountains of Lebanon and Anti-Lebanon at about 4,000 to over 6,000 feet and descending and sometimes scattering to other areas in winter.
IDENTIFICATION: The Wood Lark is a rather short-tailed, heavily streaked lark with whitish eyebrow-stripes joining on nape and with a short, thick crest, not always in evidence, and a small blackish and white mark at the edge of the wing which may show when the bird is seen on the ground at close range. In flight it differs from most larks (except Crested and Bimaculated) by showing no white at the sides of the dark tail.
NOTES: A sweet, musical 'pe-too-eet'. The song is of sweet twin notes in a descending minor key, with variations.
HABITAT: Hilly, heathy or barren places, with or without woodland.

SKY LARK *Alauda arvensis.* Length 7 in.

RANGE: The Sky Lark breeds in Europe and central Asia to the Far East and also in a small part of North Africa. In Lebanon it is a migrant and winter visitor, chiefly in the plain of Bekaa, but sometimes in the hills above and along the coastal strip. Occasionally it lingers in the Bekaa till late May, though most pass on to the breeding areas in the north. Large numbers are shot and offered for sale.
IDENTIFICATION: A mediumly large lark with longer tail than the Crested and Wood Larks, darker and more heavily streaked than Crested Lark and without the pinkish-sandy tint. It shows conspicuous white on outer tail feathers and rounded crest sometimes raised on crown but not always visible.
NOTES: Call note is a liquid twitter, the song is a joyful and sweet warbling of long duration and great variety, with many repetitions, trills and twitters.
HABITAT: It likes open grassland and agriculture.

TAWNY PIPIT *Anthus campestris*. Length 6½ in.

RANGE: Breeds around the Mediterranean and in most parts of Continental Europe and central Asia and migrates to Africa. It breeds in the mountains and foothills of Anti-Lebanon and Lebanon, and may be heard and seen in song flight in its nesting territories. It is also fairly numerous on passage, especially in autumn when I have seen fair numbers in the area of the old cedars at 6,000 and 7,000 feet.

IDENTIFICATION: A fairly large, slender, tall-standing Pipit with pale sandy plumage, without the bold, dark striations of the smaller Meadow, Tree and Red-throated Pipits. The plumage above is almost unstreaked in adults, or very softly and indistinctly marked, except on the wing which has a clear, dark-spotted wing bar. Very pale underparts have a buff wash on the upper breast, sometimes with some short, faint, dark streaks, but usually plain in adults, and the flanks are also washed with buff. There is a distinct creamy eye-brow-stripe. The tail and flight-feathers are dark with contrasting pale edges, the outer tail-feathers showing some buff-white in the spread tail. The fairly long legs are yellow to flesh-colour. Immature plumage is more mottled above and streaked on the breast.

NOTES: A loud 'tzeet' call note, with variations. Song on the wing, 'cherra-ki, cherra-ki, cherra-ki', keeping time with each opening of the wings in gradually rising flight; sometimes speeding up as the bird planes down to the ground with stiff wings and raised tail; or a vibrant, loud 'chur-vee chur-vee chur-vee', often shrill and metallic.

HABITAT: As above.

LONG-BILLED PIPIT *Anthus similis*. Length $6\frac{3}{4}$–$7\frac{1}{2}$ in.

RANGE: Breeds in southern mid-Asia westward to the Levant, and in parts of Africa. It appears to summer in the mountains here and to wander to lower levels in the southern part of its range in winter.
IDENTIFICATION: This is the largest Pipit in the Middle East, larger than the Tawny Pipit, and usually a quiet and often solitary bird. It is distinguished from the Tawny Pipit by the much less sandy plumage with less clear cut wing and tail patterns and less conspicuous pale eyebrow-stripe. Some eastern and southern races are rather dark, with a russet wash beneath and brown above, but the bird of Lebanon, Syria and Palestine to the Jordan valley, is pale greyish-brown with pale buff or pale cream underparts, almost unspotted or faintly spotted in adult plumage, and only softly patterned above, with a longish tail and fairly long, powerful bill. The tail is brown with paler edgings and with pale buff on the outer tail-feathers. The legs are dull yellowish, flesh, or tan to light brown; not to be confused with the dark brown legs of the Water Pipit. Immature plumage is more mottled above and streaked on the breast.
NOTES: A quiet bird, but in spring I have heard a loud, short, plaintive note, and a soft, clear, high 'pweep', followed by a faint 'pi-pi-pi' from one of a pair carrying some fine grass for nesting. One bird had a short song, 'twer-twee-twer' repeated, sometimes from a rock but usually while taking short song-flights. At other times the song recalls that of the Rock Pipit, being a repetition of 'chwee-chwee-chwee-chwee . . .' as I heard it in south Lebanon in early May. 'Call, a loud chirrup and the song is described as an unmusical "kliddh-kliddh" or "chwee-chwa-chwee-chwa" while soaring' (C. Benson). 'Soaring up a few feet excitedly and parachuting back to earth . . . a single note, "tseep", is repeated at short intervals, sometimes higher, sometimes lower in key' (Salim Ali). A sweet song is described in Socotra Island. (Mackworth-Praed & Grant.)
HABITAT: Arid, rocky hillsides.

TREE PIPIT *Anthus trivialis*. Length 6 in.

RANGE: Breeds in Europe and central Asia north of Lebanon and winters in Africa. In Lebanon it is seen on passage in both directions, from sea level to 6,000 feet in the old cedars.
IDENTIFICATION: Light brown with blackish striations above and beneath. The buffish-white underparts are washed with a yellow tint on the throat, breast and flanks. Usually slightly less densely streaked with slightly bolder streaks than Meadow Pipit. Both show conspicuous white on outer tail-feathers. Leg-colour is pinker in Tree Pipit and more tan in Meadow Pipit, and the latter has a much longer hind claw. Recognized by its perching on bushes, telephone wires and trees, especially on passage, and by 'teeze' note.
NOTES: A high wheezy squeak, 'teeze'. The song is more musical than that of most Pipits, some part being similar to the Wood Lark's. One version of this is, 'pit-pit-pit-pit-dear-dear-sweet-sweet-sweet', drawn out to a slow, lingering end. The bird may sing short phrases from a tree but has a distinctive parachute display song-flight starting from a perch and landing on a perch again, or sometimes on the ground. Unlikely to sing on passage.
HABITAT: Rough ground anywhere from the bushes of Ammiq Swamp and the coastal strip to the highest cedars.

1.

2.

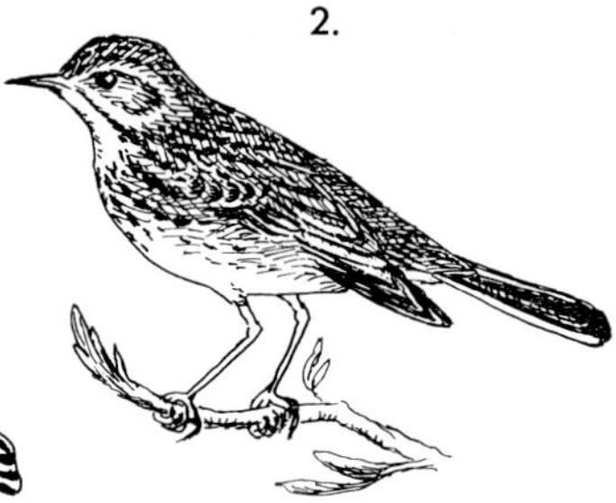

1 Tawny Pipit. 2. Tree Pipit.

MEADOW PIPIT *Anthus pratensis*. Length $5\frac{3}{4}$ in.

RANGE: A migrant here, and a winter visitor as well. Its breeding range is in central and northern Europe eastward to Russia, and it winters as far south as North Africa.

IDENTIFICATION: Very like Tree Pipit, light yellowish brown, densely striated above and beneath. (See Tree Pipit.)

NOTES: A sharp 'peep, peep, peep', alarm and flight note, and a quiet 'pipit' only heard from birds on the ground. The song is usually in flight, starting with 'psip-psip-psip' and running into a squeaky trill of 'ipipipipip' as the bird planes steeply to the ground with raised tail. Unlikely to sing in Lebanon.

HABITAT: Grassy places (if any) and anywhere along the coastal strip, in the Bekaa and at Ammiq Swamp. Not seen on high mountains.

1. Meadow Pipit. 2. Red-Throated Pipit, winter. 2A. summer. 3. Water Pipit, summer. 3A. winter.

RED-THROATED PIPIT *Anthus cervinus*. Length $5\frac{3}{4}$ in. Page 105

RANGE: Breeds in the extreme north of Europe and Asia and is not uncommon on passage, chiefly near the coast, also at Ammiq Swamp.
IDENTIFICATION: Not unlike the last two species but the blackish striations are much bolder and heavier above and below contrasting more conspicuously with whitish underparts. The rump too is boldly streaked. In breeding plumage the throat and upper breast are washed with rosy rust-red.
NOTES: A high nasal, ringing 'peet', a nasal, wheezy squeak, 'zeeez', a short pleasant musical 'choop', and others.
HABITAT: Specially likes wet grassland, also swamps, marshes, and in Lebanon, the coast.

WATER PIPIT *Anthus spinoletta*. Length $6\frac{1}{2}$ in. Page 105

RANGE: The Water Pipit has a wide range though it is very local in habitat. The species is divided into two groups of races, the Water Pipit group being chiefly found inland in mountainous regions in parts of Europe and Asia and in a large range across North America; and the Rock Pipit group (subspecies) being chiefly confined to sea coasts in western and northern Europe. The race of Water Pipit said to pass through Lebanon on passage is of a palish grey above.
IDENTIFICATION: Larger than the three foregoing Pipits, light grey-brown to grey above and nearly white to pinkish-buff on the breast. There is a whitish eyebrow-stripe and white outer tail-feathers, and the general effect is somewhat wagtail-like. In autumn the pinkish tone is lost and the breast is streaked. The legs are dark.
NOTES: A loud alarm or flight note, 'pseep', often repeated several times. Song (unusual on passage) variable, often similar to the Tree Pipit's without the lingering last notes, or it may recall Meadow Pipit's.
HABITAT: A mountain bird, but in winter it likes the vicinity of water and marshes.

YELLOW WAGTAIL *Motacilla flava*. Length $6\frac{1}{2}$ in.

RANGE: Breeds throughout Europe, a large part of Asia to extreme north-west America, and around the Mediterranean. European and western Asian races chiefly winter in Africa, some also in India. Abundant on passage in Lebanon, the Black-headed race, *M.f. feldegg*, may attempt breeding.
IDENTIFICATION: This species is divided into many races with fairly distinct differences in plumage. All have yellow underparts in spring plumage, with olive-yellowish-green upperparts and black tails with white outer feathers. Longish, thin tails swaying up and down as the slender birds run about: this is typical of all Wagtails. The Black-headed Yellow Wagtail, the race breeding in the Lebanon area, has a glossy black head in breeding plumage. Female, autumn and immature plumages all show brown mottlings on black heads, browner backs, and faded yellow underparts. Young show an indistinct bib-line. The race, *M.f. flava*, the Blue-headed Wagtail, has a slate-blue head, darker on the cheeks, with long, bold, white eye-stripe, and breeds chiefly in Europe. The Grey-headed race, *M.f. thumbergi*, has a very dark grey head with blackish cheeks and usually no trace of eye-stripe, and breeds in Scandinavia and north-west Asia. These two are seen on passage to and from wintering areas. The Yellow Wagtail race, *M.f. flavissima*, breeds chiefly in Great Britain and is unlikely to occur here, but a rather similar race with a very yellow head, *M.f. lutea*, from east to mid Russia, migrates in the Levant area and might occur. (See also Citrine Wagtail, page 206.) Most of these races, however, are indistinguishable in the field except males in breeding plumage.
NOTES: A high 'tseep' or 'tsee-eep'.
HABITAT: The habitat on passage is chiefly coastal and through the plain of Bekaa. Found near water, in flat areas and in cultivation. Very great numbers are shot.

GREY WAGTAIL *Motacilla cinerea*. Length 7 in.

RANGE: Lebanon lies on the southern limit of the breeding range through much of Europe and Asia. It is not common here, though it appears to breed very locally in the mountains, and a few are seen along the shore from late October to March.
IDENTIFICATION: A graceful, long-tailed wagtail with yellow underparts, blue-grey back and head with white superciliary-stripe, yellowish rump and black tail with white outer feathers. The flight feathers are blackish with pale edges, and the male has a short black bib on the throat in breeding plumage. Winter males, females and young birds are less slaty above, greenish-grey to brownish-grey, and have whitish throats and paler yellow to buff-white underparts with bright yellow only under the tail.
NOTES: 'tseeseep' or 'sreep'. The song is a pretty warbling, sweeter and more varied than that of other wagtails.
HABITAT: In the breeding season it is found in or near mountain streams. In winter some descend to coastal rivers and a few occasionally to streams or swamps in the Bekaa.

1. Yellow Wagtail, Black-headed race. 1A. Blue-headed. 1B. Grey-headed. 1C. *M.f. lutea* (with yellow head). 2. Grey Wagtail. 2A. male, summer.

WHITE WAGTAIL *Motacilla alba.* Length 7 in.

RANGE: Lebanon lies on the southern fringe of the main breeding range, which is almost throughout Europe and Asia. Summering birds are fairly common and breeding has been claimed from time to time. It is not uncommon on passage and in winter.
IDENTIFICATION: A slender, black and white bird, with undulating flight, as with other wagtails, and dainty walking or short, fast running with tail swaying up and down when the bird is on the ground. It is always busy snatching at insects.

The slender tail is black with white outer feathers as with other wagtails, and there is a deep black bib from chin to breast. The mantle is grey. In winter the throat is whitish with only a crescent or narrow bib of black. Young in autumn have a slight yellowish wash on white parts and a narrower, smudgy, brownish bib-line.
NOTES: 'terreep', 'chizzeek', etc. The song is a fast, cheerful warble.
HABITAT: The bed of streams and rivers on gravel or mud, or by any inland water or marsh, in fields, agriculture, farms or gardens or any places where soft insects can be found.

RED-BACKED SHRIKE *Lanius collurio*. Length 6¾ in.

RANGE: Lebanon lies on the southern fringe of the breeding range right through Europe and Asia, and nesting here is doubtful, though the species has been described as a summer resident. Migrants are seen in May and reappear in summer and autumn on their way to winter quarters in East Africa.

IDENTIFICATION: The male has a chestnut back, light blue-grey head, nape and rump, black tail with some white on the basal half of the outer feathers, black ear-coverts and whitish underparts washed pale pink on the breast. The female is red-brown, pale beneath with some fine, crescent-shaped barring below, which can only be seen at close range. Immature birds are similar but show the crescent-barring all over the plumage. The bill is slightly hooked at the tip. The bird usually perches on a bush or small tree watching for prey. Shrikes prey chiefly on small birds, large insects, especially grass-hoppers, also lizards and small rodents, often impaling their surplus catches on thorns.

NOTES: There are various harsh notes, including 'chack, chack', and the song is a pretty, fast warbling.

HABITAT: It may be seen anywhere in Lebanon, but chiefly in the mountains and the coastal area, on bushes, trees, scrub, ruins or walls.

A.

B.

A. male.

B. female.

MASKED SHRIKE *Lanius nubicus.* Length $6\frac{3}{4}$ in.

RANGE: The comparatively small breeding range is from parts of Greece and Bulgaria, throughout Turkey eastward and southward to the Persian Gulf, including Syria, Lebanon and Cyprus to Jordan and Palestine. In Lebanon, some breed in the hills and many more are seen on passage.

IDENTIFICATION: It is the smallest and most black-and-white of the Levant Shrikes, with a longer tail than the others. The crown, nape, back, rump and tail are black, with white forehead, scapulars, wing-patches and outer tail-feathers. Underparts are white with an orange wash on sides of breast and flanks. In flight (and also when perched) it shows a white bar on the fore-wing and a long white patch on either side of the back formed by the white scapulars. This is the same pattern as that of the Woodchat Shrike, but without the latter's chestnut-red crown and nape and showy white rump. The sexes are similar.

NOTES: Harsh and plaintive. The song is usually a quiet, pleasant warble, but sometimes a dry, toneless, scratchy one.

HABITAT: Bushes, trees, tall scrub, olives, chiefly in the hills.

WOODCHAT SHRIKE *Lanius senator*. Length 6¾ in.

RANGE: Breeds in Europe and all Mediterranean regions including the Levant; eastward to Caspian area and south-eastward along the eastern side of the Persian Gulf; also in parts of Africa. European birds are seen on passage but the local breeding race is said to be *L.s. niloticus*, with more white in the wing and a broad band of white at the base of the tail.

IDENTIFICATION: Similar in colour-pattern to the Masked Shrike but with rather more white in the wings and scapulars and a conspicuous white rump and outer tail feathers of the black tail; also with chestnut or orange-red crown and nape and white underparts, and the forehead is black as well as the ear-coverts. It perches rather upright in the open on a bush or tree and is a stouter bird than the Masked and larger-headed. Immature birds are like young Red-backed Shrikes, but have pale scapulars and rump.

NOTES: Harsh notes or chatter and a pretty warbling song which is often prolonged.

HABITAT: Gardens, orchards, trees, olive groves and bushes, also in mountain scrub.

1. Woodchat Shrike. 2. Lesser Grey Shrike. 3. Great Grey Shrike.

LESSER GREY SHRIKE *Lanius minor*. Length 8 in.

RANGE: The breeding range extends across most of Europe to mid Asia, including Syria and Lebanon. However, nesting here is not proved, though a few birds have been seen in the summer months. It is also seen on passage from time to time.
IDENTIFICATION: Pure light grey above and whitish, often washed with pale pink beneath, with black wings showing broad white wing-bars or patches, and black tail with white on the outer feathers. It has black ear-coverts, and in spring a black forehead joining with the black on the sides of the head. Most safely distinguished from *L. excubitor* by this broad band of black covering the forehead in spring, but this is lost in autumn. It tends to perch more upright than *L. excubitor* on telegraph wires and high perches in the open. Young birds of both species are brownish or brownish-grey with inconspicuous barring, soon lost as they moult into a plain brownish-grey plumage.
NOTES: Harsh, chattering notes. The song is a low, prolonged warbling. Habitat and predatory habits as other shrikes.

GREAT GREY SHRIKE *Lanius excubitor*. Length 9½ in.

RANGE: Rather scarce on passage. The breeding range extends all round the northern hemisphere and into Africa, but breeding has been reported only occasionally in Lebanon.
IDENTIFICATION: Similar to *L. minor*, but the underparts of some races are washed pinkish-grey or grey. The Lebanon race is greyish-white beneath with a very narrow black band on the forehead over the bill, but this is not conspicuous enough to cause confusion with *L. minor* and the species can usually be distinguished by its larger size, white eyebrow streak, much more white on the scapulars, and low, usually undulating flight with upward sweep to perch. For juvenile plumage, see *L. minor* above. Notes and habitat also as above.

GOLDEN ORIOLE *Oriolus oriolus*. Length $9\frac{1}{2}$ in.

RANGE: The breeding range lies across most of Europe and a large part of Asia. This beautiful bird is often seen here, sometimes in good numbers on passage, especially through the Bekaa area, where it is shot almost to the last bird in the tall trees only to be found in and around the villages and towns. It is reported to breed in south Lebanon.

IDENTIFICATION: Rather the shape of a Starling but larger, smoother, more streamlined. The male is vivid crocus yellow with black wings and tail, the latter with yellow ends to the outer feathers. There is a black stripe from the red bill to the red eye. Female and immature birds are more or less bright yellowish-green, brightest green on the head and mantle, yellowest on the rump and flanks and under the tail, and greyish-white on the throat and breast, with pinkish-red bills and brown to crimson eyes. Wings and tail are darker, the latter becoming blackish with yellow corners as with the male.

NOTES: Best recognized by the male's loud, clear, contralto whistle of 'hoola-weeoo', sometimes rendered 'who-are-you-oo?'

There are also surprisingly harsh, churring and grating notes and one recalling the Green Woodpecker's yaffle.

HABITAT: The foliage of trees, often tall trees, preferably near water.

ROSE-COLOURED STARLING *Sturnus roseus*. Length 8½ in. Page 116

RANGE: Breeds from south-east Europe to mid Asia, largely north and east of Lebanon. It was supposed to be breeding here in times past, but there seem to be no certain recent records. As in other countries, it appears to be a late and very erratic spring and summer vagrant and is occasional till late autumn.

IDENTIFICATION: A sturdy, rather short-tailed bird with plumage of boldly contrasting light pink with a glossy black head, crest, neck, wings and tail. The crest sweeps back over the nape; the bill is pinkish. Young birds are light brown with pale brownish-white underparts and yellowish-brown bills. In winter, adult plumage is partly obscured by light brown tips and the bill is brownish.

NOTES: Some of the notes are similar to the Starling's, as is the habitat.

STARLING *Sturnus vulgaris*. Length 8½ in. Page 116

RANGE: Breeds in Europe and a large part of Asia. Said to have bred here, but there are no written records. However, it is a passage migrant and a common winter visitor, and flocks are often seen in the Bekaa in mid-winter.

IDENTIFICATION: A short blackish bird, glossed with green, purple and bronze and in winter thickly speckled with small white spots. The bill is dark, becoming yellow or yellowish in summer. Young birds are dull brown, very pale on the throat, and in autumn blackish plumage with conspicuous white spots first starts to appear on the underparts.

NOTES: It has various churrs and chatters and harsh alarm notes, and often mimics other birds in song which includes bubbling, clicking and sweet whistles.

HABITAT: Both this and the Rose-coloured Starling usually frequent agriculture, plains and open country. They are gregarious, forming flocks in winter, waddling and running on the ground, sometimes hopping, in search of food.

JAY *Garrulus glandarius*. Length 13½ in.

RANGE: The breeding range includes nearly all Europe and a large part of Asia, also an area in north-west Africa. The race *G.g. atricapillus*, resident in Lebanon, has a black crown. It is not uncommon in the hills and many are shot and offered for sale.
IDENTIFICATION: A bird the size of a pigeon; body plumage pinkish sandy brown, darkest on the back, with wide black 'moustaches' and a black, bushy crown or crest with whitish forehead, cheeks and throat. The wings show a white patch and the wing-coverts are bright blue finely barred with black. The conspicuous white rump contrasting with the black tail catches the eye as the bird flies away. It is shy and cautious and quickly takes cover.
NOTES: Usually a loud, harsh, grating screech. Sometimes a mewing note and others.
HABITAT: Woods, plantations, trees and scrub anywhere in the lower mountains and hills.

1. Starling, winter. 2. Rose-coloured Starling. 3. Jay (black-crowned race).

CHOUGH *Pyrrhocorax pyrrhocorax*. Length 15½ in.

ALPINE CHOUGH *Pyrrhocorax graculus*. Length 15 in.

RANGE: Both these birds have a scattered breeding range through the mountains of southern Europe and mid to south Asia. They also breed in extreme north-west Africa and some of the islands of the Mediterranean. A few Choughs also remain on the west coasts of the British Isles and Ireland. In Lebanon their status is uncertain. The latest records of each species are in 1963 of a flock of Alpine Choughs at the highest point of the Lebanon range, and in 1969 of a flock of Choughs near Faraya, but there have been no very recent breeding records of either.
IDENTIFICATION: Both birds are black, like very small Ravens and a little larger than Jackdaws. The Chough is more greenish-black and has red legs and down-curved red bill. The Alpine Chough's bill is shorter and yellow. The legs are also red.
NOTES: Various. The Chough's are usually 'chuff' and a ringing 'chee-aw', and the Alpine Chough's are thinner, less clarion cries.
HABITAT: Mountains, cliffs, sometimes ravines. The Alpine Chough stays chiefly at high altitudes.

JACKDAW *Corvus monedula*. Length 13 in.

RANGE: Breeds from mid to west Asia and in most of Europe, also in extreme north-west Africa. Lebanon lies on the southern border of its breeding range, and it is mainly known here as a winter visitor, flocking, especially in the Bekaa plain and Anti-Lebanon during late autumn and winter months.
IDENTIFICATION: The Jackdaw is a little smaller than the Choughs, and greyer, especially on the nape and sides of the neck which are very light in contrast to the black forehead and face.
NOTES: Has a lively vocabulary of 'jack' and 'jack-a-jack', and a harsh grating alarm.
HABITAT: Above.

HOODED CROW *Corvus corone cornix*. Length 18½ in.

RANGE: Breeds in large areas of Asia and Europe, also in Egypt, Mediterranean islands and the Levant. In Lebanon it is both a migrant and resident, breeding very thinly here and there chiefly in the mountains and hills and occasionally flocking in autumn and winter. It is even seen on passage frequenting the old Cedars at 6,000 feet.
IDENTIFICATION: The Crow is much larger than the foregoing members of this family and has a lightish grey or putty grey body and black head, bib, wings, tail, legs and bill.
NOTES: A harsh croak and variations. No special habitat.

RAVEN *Corvus corax*. Length 25 in.

RANGE: Worldwide in four continents. In Lebanon it is a resident of the summits and wilder mountains and also sometimes of ravines. Nests have been recorded occasionally.
IDENTIFICATION: The largest of the Crow family with slower, more powerful flight, sometimes gliding or soaring, or rolling in courtship flights; occasionally flying upside down during rolling display. The plumage, legs and great heavy bill are black. Recognized by large size, all black plumage and by the great bill and wedge-tipped tail seen in flight.
NOTES: A deep 'Pork, pork', a short, higher, horn-like metallic note and other croaks and chuckles.
HABITAT: As above.

1. Alpine Chough. 2. Chough. 3. Magpie. 4. Jackdaw. 5. Hooded Crow. 6. Raven.

AFRICAN or YELLOW-VENTED BULBUL

Pycnonotus barbatus. Length about 8½ in.

RANGE: The breeding range of the African Bulbul, where it is also resident, is in Africa, Arabia and the Levant. The race which is resident in Lebanon is *P.b. xanthopygos* and differs from many others in being bright yellow from vent to under tail-coverts and by having a narrow wattle round the eye.

IDENTIFICATION: The Bulbul may be the favourite bird of Lebanon, chiefly as a songster and also as a familiar local resident. It is about the shape of a Blackbird but is smaller and has a slightly shorter tail, while the steep crown and slightly shaggy throat are quite different. The head and throat are black, shading into dull olive-brown on the back with a slightly more sandy tint on the rump, the black throat shading into the brownish-grey underparts. The wings are dark brown, the tail brownish-black and beneath the tail is bright yellow. The bill, slightly down-curved at the tip, is black with grey at the base. The birds pair for life and are sociable, sometimes meeting in small, noisy parties, usually soon after dawn, to chatter excitedly with much minor activity.

NOTES: The notes are chattering and churring; the song varied, sometimes rich and flute-like, sometimes like the Blackbird's contralto whistle but lower, sometimes husky and deep, nearly always in short disjointed snatches. Occasionally other birds are mimicked, especially the Thrush Nightingale, Oriole and Blackbird. It sings all the year round.

HABITAT: Gardens, orchards, groves, thickets, trees and bushes anywhere, chiefly in the coastal strip and at no great altitude. It is common in the gardens of Beirut, and in orange and banana groves.

DIPPER *Cinclus cinclus*. Length 7 in.

RANGE: The race which is resident in Lebanon, and apparently only here, is *C.c. rufiventris*, with pale rufous or rusty abdomen. Other races of this species breed in Europe, Asia, two or three spots in extreme North Africa and some Mediterranean islands.
IDENTIFICATION: A short, plump bird with a short tail, in shape like a giant Wren, with blackish back, white breast and rusty abdomen. The short tail is often cocked up as the bird bobs up and down, dipping and curtseying on a boulder or rock in some rapid, mountain torrent. It feeds chiefly underwater, walking about on the bed of a stream or swimming beneath the surface.
NOTES: A quiet bird; occasionally a short note is heard in flight. The song is a rapid warbling, sometimes imitative, to be heard at any season but chiefly in winter.
HABITAT: Mountain streams, waterfalls, and rocky rivers chiefly on the west side of the Lebanon range.

WREN *Troglodytes troglodytes*. Length $3\frac{3}{4}$ in.

RANGE: It breeds right round the world and is largely resident in Europe, a few places in extreme North Africa and parts of Asia and North America. In Lebanon it is a resident chiefly of river gorges in the Lebanon range from sea level to higher mountain ravines.
IDENTIFICATION: A very small russet-brown bird, with short tail often cocked up, dipping, bobbing, scolding, or flying straight and low (without undulations) with fast vibrating wings from one point of cover to another. It is usually out of sight, creeping in foliage. At close quarters it is seen to be softly barred nearly all over.
NOTES: A loud ticking note and harsh churring. Sings almost all the year round, a shrill, loud, clear, beautiful song, full of trills and exuberance.
HABITAT: Moist thickets, tangled shrubs and creepers, thick herbage, gardens, river-side cover, plantations, etc.

SIBERIAN ACCENTOR *Prunella montanella.*

One record. Vagrant from Siberia. Male dark, streaked red-brown above, greyish rump, black crown and cheeks with wide yellow-ochre eyebrow stripe and area below black ear-coverts, merging into warm buff underparts. Female duller, paler.

DUNNOCK *Prunella modularis.* Page 160

A few winter records in Lebanon. Breeds further north.
Sparrow-size, but has a grey breast and sides of head, thin bill (unlike Sparrows') and a streaked brown back. It moves about quietly in cultivation, flower-beds and undergrowth, and has a shrill, squeaky note and short, high, cheerful, jingling song like part of the Wren's, but less musical.

Wren.

CETTI'S WARBLER *Cettia cetti*. Length $5\frac{1}{2}$ in.

RANGE: The breeding range, where it is resident except in the eastern part, surrounds the Mediterranean, eastward to mid Asia. In Lebanon it breeds in western river valleys and, apparently, in ravines in the mountains, the Ammiq Swamp and other similar habitat.

IDENTIFICATION: A secretive, darkish-chestnut-brown bird skulking in thick waterside cover and seldom seen. Underparts pale, nearly white. The rounded tail is sometimes cocked up. The loud gush of song is the usual indication of the bird's presence.

NOTES: Several short, loud and soft notes and a scolding churr. The song is an abrupt, loud gush, stopping as suddenly as it started, and usually at long intervals: a clear, high, penetrating, 'Chiweechiweechiweechiweeoo', or 'cheewoocheewoocheewoo'.

HABITAT: Tangled thickets and vegetation near streams, ditches, marshes, swamps, and rivers.

1. Cetti's Warbler. 2. Savi's Warbler. 3. Moustached Warbler. 4. Sedge Warbler. 5. Reed Warbler. 6. Great Reed Warbler.

SAVI'S WARBLER *Locustella luscinioides*. Length $5\frac{1}{2}$ in.

RANGE: The breeding range is in Europe, mid Asia, some of the Mediterranean countries and an area of North Africa. Though breeding in lakes north and south of Lebanon, it was not recorded here until May 1965 when I found it, apparently breeding, or attempting to breed, in a reed-bed of Ammiq Swamp. Here, at least three birds were singing and evidently in established breeding territories. On my next visit in April 1969 I found ten, or more, singing, each in its own area of reeds during my two days' watching. Certainly they must breed here. There are also two autumn records of single migrants in Septembers 1963 and 1964, one in central Lebanon and one further north by a river.
IDENTIFICATION: A smooth-looking, unstreaked, reddish-brown warbler, with pale underparts slightly tinted with rust on the flanks and breast, and with a rather wide, fair-lengthed, rounded tail. It is usually unseen in reeds or bushes, but will sing from a reed in full view, when the reeling song at once identifies it as it turns its head from side to side in a cricket-like whirring song.
NOTES: Often silent, but sometimes chatters and scolds. The song is like the whirr of a fisherman's reel turning, or some other mechanical device. It is not unlike that of the Grasshopper Warbler, but louder, deeper and less continuous. Some insects make a similar sound, which may be the reason why the species has been overlooked hitherto.
HABITAT: Swamps, reed-beds, willows and other bushes in or by fresh water.

MOUSTACHED WARBLER *Lusciniola melanopogon.*
Length 5 in.

SEDGE WARBLER *Acrocephalus schoenobaenus.* Page 123
Length 5 in.

RANGE: The former breeds chiefly along northern coasts of the Mediterranean and south-eastern Europe eastward toward mid Asia and in north-east Tunisia. Though apparently unrecorded previously in Lebanon, I found a pair probably attempting to breed in Ammiq Swamp in 1965, and at least two males singing there in 1969. It was recorded in Palestine in the nineteen fifties and in Jordan in 1963. The Sedge Warbler breeds in Europe and eastward to north and mid Asia and locally in north-west Africa. In Lebanon it is only known as a spring migrant. Breeding is not proved here, so far south of its normal range, despite late spring and summer records.
IDENTIFICATION: The two species are somewhat similar, both are boldly streaked above, with pale, buff-white underparts and a conspicuous pale superciliary-stripe contrasting with darker crown. However, the Moustached is seen to have a blackish crown instead of a streaked brown one; a clear-cut white superciliary-stripe instead of a merging pale buff one; a red-brown tint instead of a sandy yellowish-tawny one; a white throat, darker brown cheeks, and a habit of cocking the tail.
NOTES: The Sedge Warbler has a varied rapid, exhuberant song of harsh, squeaky notes, sweet twitters and trills; that of the Moustached Warbler is less rapid and excited than the former's, sweeter than the Reed Warbler's, with occasional Nightingale-like crescendo repetitions of a high note, or a repeated plaintive one. Both have short, scolding, notes, churring or ticking.
HABITAT: Chiefly reed-beds, especially the Moustached. The Sedge Warbler prefers the outskirts with aquatic vegetation, ditches and marshes with thick herbage.

MARSH WARBLER *Acrocephalus palustris.*

So far, one autumn and one spring record only. Breeds to the north and winters in Africa. Like Reed Warbler, but more olive, less warm in tone, throat whiter, cheeks and round the eye paler, and legs flesh pink instead of dark. The song, which is heard from spring to autumn, is quite different from Reed Warbler's. It is very sweet, gushing and varied, including snatches mimicking other birds, e.g., Goldfinch, Lark and Canary trills, and the chatterings of other Warbler's, with some harsh notes as with Sedge Warbler.

REED WARBLER *Acrocephalus scirpaceus.* Pages 123, 160

Length 5 in.

GREAT REED WARBLER *Acrocephalus arundinaceus* Page 123

Length $7\frac{1}{2}$ in.

RANGE: Both breed in Europe and from parts of west to mid Asia, and along the Mediterranean coasts. In the Lebanon both appear to breed, when unmolested, in Ammiq Swamp. They were almost certainly doing so in 1965. The former has also been recorded once in winter, and both may be seen on passage to and from winter quarters in Africa.

IDENTIFICATION: Both have smooth, unstreaked plumage, brown above and buffish-white beneath. The Great Reed Warbler may be distinguished by its size, looking twice as large as any other reed-loving warbler (except Clamorous Warbler),* and by the loud, strident song, powerful bill and clearer buff superciliary-stripe than that of the Reed Warbler.

NOTES: The Reed Warbler's song is rather slower than the Sedge-Warbler's, more repetitive, a measured 'chirrick-chirrick-chirrick, jik-jik, chuck-chuck-chuck', etc. The Great Reed Warbler's has similar phrases, though louder, harsher and deeper, interspersed with frog-like croaks; a slower, more disjointed, 'crarck-crarck-jagger-jagger', etc.

HABITAT: Reed-beds. The Great Reed Warbler sings from an exposed position on a reed, sometimes the Reed Warbler does the same, but it is usually skulking out of sight in or near reed-beds, in ditches or swamps, occasionally in cultivation.

* See page 207.

ICTERINE WARBLER *Hippolais icterina*. Length $5\frac{1}{4}$ in.

RANGE: Breeds from mid to north-west Asia and in Europe, and is seen in Lebanon only as a migrant, usually in autumn. I have seen it in spring also, but there are no recent breeding records.

IDENTIFICATION: Like others of the genus Hippolais, this is a fairly solid-looking yet very streamlined warbler, slightly long-headed, with longer, less slender bill than the leaf-warblers, and tapering, round-tipped tail. It often shows a high, bushy forehead, or may look flat headed. Usually it may be distinguished from the others by all yellow underparts and more yellowish-olive or greenish-olive upperparts. (See Olive-Tree, Upcher's, Olivaceous, and Booted Warblers.)

NOTES: Churring 'tick' and 'chack' notes. The song is varied and often includes mimicry, with sweet warbling and harsh, repeated phrases.

HABITAT: Chiefly in the foliage of trees.

1. Icterine Warbler. 2. Olive-Tree Warbler. 3. Olivaceous Warbler. 4. Booted Warbler.

 Page 161

UPCHER'S WARBLER *Hippolais languida*

Length about $5\frac{1}{4}$ in.

RANGE: The breeding range is from the Levant eastward into Asia, and it certainly breeds in fair numbers in Lebanon, chiefly in the hills, up to 5,000 feet or above.
IDENTIFICATION: As with other *Hippolais* warblers, it is rather grey, with purer, darkish grey (not diluted with brownish and olive) head, cheeks and ear-coverts and rather paler grey rump contrasting with darker tail. Underparts are whitish as with the Olive-Tree Warbler. Unlike the others, it cocks its tail well up as well as showing the slight flicking movement which is usual with this genus, especially with the Olivaceous Warbler.
NOTES: 'Chack, chack' and 'tick' notes. The song is loud, very varied, pleasant and musical.
HABITAT: Chiefly in bushes in the hills.

OLIVE-TREE WARBLER *Hippolais olivetorum.* Page 127

Length 6 in.

RANGE: Breeds only in countries around the east Mediterranean, but there are no recent breeding records for Lebanon and records of single birds may have been migrants.
IDENTIFICATION: Having the general characteristics of the genus, mentioned under Icterine Warbler, it is distinguished from the others by its larger size, like a very large Olivaceous, but greyer and much less uniform.
NOTES: A rich, loud, pleasant Sedge-Warbler-like song, though deeper. Other notes and habitat as Icterine Warbler.
HABITAT: The foliage of trees, olive groves and bushes.

OLIVACEOUS WARBLER *Hippolais pallida*
Length $5\frac{1}{4}$ in.

RANGE: Breeds here, and in many Mediterranean countries, including Africa, from Spain eastward towards south and mid Asia. It is a summer visitor to Lebanon.
IDENTIFICATION: The general characteristics are as other *Hippolais* Warblers. The upperparts are olive-brown to greyish-brown with slightly darker wings and tail, the latter having whitish outer-feathers (*seldom visible*, as also in the case of the Booted and other members of this genus). It habitually flicks the tail slightly while feeding. This is a slight down-and-back flicker and does not include tail-cocking. (See Upcher's Warbler.) The thin, whitish eye-ring is also a feature shared by other members of the genus. Underparts are dirty-whitish.
NOTES: Like those of other *Hippolais* Warblers. The song is a rather dry, often hurried and rambling, repetitive warble.
HABITAT: Thickets, trees, bushes, gardens, groves and cultivation.

BOOTED WARBLER *Hippolais caligata*. Length $4\frac{1}{2}$ in. Page 127

RANGE: Breeds from north-west Asia eastward to the Yenisey area of Russia, and south to Pakistan, and was not recorded in Lebanon until 1964 when one was studied closely in a tree by the Beirut river on 30 April. In 1965 two more were seen probably of this species. Sight records may be doubtful owing to possible confusion with a very small race of Olivaceous Warbler found to be on passage with them in Jordan recently. Migration was thought to be no further west than India and southern Arabia, but has been seen passing through Jordan since 1963 and probably passes through Lebanon almost unnoticed.
IDENTIFICATION: Looks very small for a *Hippolais* Warbler and more like a *Phylloscopus* (leaf warbler), having a shorter bill and usually a more brownish tint than the rest of the group, with whitish underparts washed with buff at the sides or with greyish. The eye looks beady, picked out by the paler eye-ring, and the round-ended tail is rather short and slightly tapering. Legs, instead of being greyish to dark slate-blue as with most others of the group, are pale, from dull ochre to light greyish-brown.
NOTES: The song is said to be cheerful, often rapid with some sweet notes. Call notes are 'teck, teck', and other ticking or scolding sounds like those of the other members of the genus.
HABITAT: Trees, gardens, bushes, scrub and low cover near water.

BARRED WARBLER *Sylvia nisoria.* Length 6 in.

RANGE: The breeding range in Europe and Asia is north of Lebanon. Here it is not uncommon on passage, and sometimes plentiful in spring.
IDENTIFICATION: A fairly large greyish warbler with a fair length of tail, skulking and shy, but not quick-moving; will sometimes remain in the open long enough for observation in detail. The whitish underparts are barred with fine, dark-grey crescent-marks, but these are very hard to see except at reasonably close range, and immature birds lack them entirely. The adult has a conspicuous yellow eye. The upperparts are brownish-grey with darker wings, and the tail which is often flicked sometimes shows a little white at the sides, sometimes at the tips of the outer feathers only. Characteristically it glides from one perch to another.
NOTES: Low harsh notes, churring and chacking. The song is a fairly loud, deep, rapid warble resembling that of the Garden Warbler but lower and of much shorter duration.
HABITAT: Thorn bushes and scrub, small trees and bushes in green, moist places, thickets, agriculture.

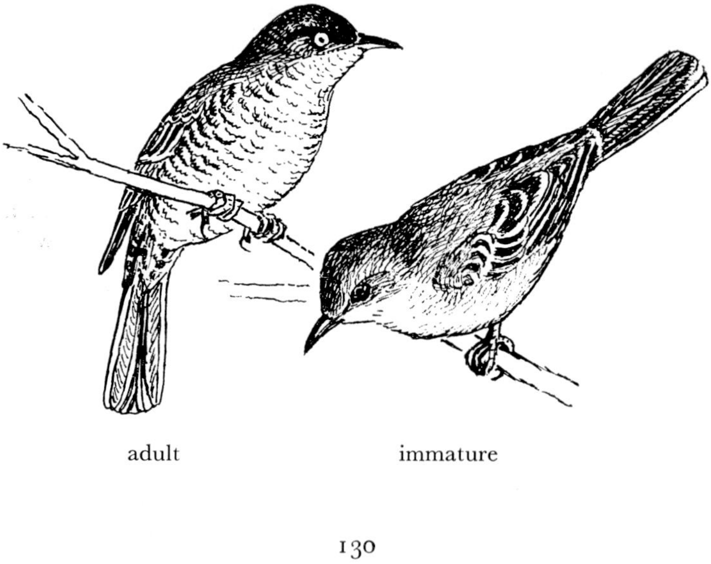

adult immature

ORPHEAN WARBLER *Sylvia hortensis*. Length 6 in.

RANGE: It breeds in the countries round the Mediterranean eastward to southern central Asia. In Lebanon it is a summer visitor and migrant, wintering in Africa, Arabia and India, and nests here from the mountains and hills down to sea level.
IDENTIFICATION: The Orphean Warbler is a beautiful songster heard in the river valleys and mountains. It is rather a large Warbler. The male has a blackish head merging into the grey-brown of the mantle, a white throat and underparts, the latter washed with pale pink-buff, and a striking pale yellow or whitish eye. The grey-brown tail has white on the outer feathers. The blackish shade of the rather high crown, cheeks and ear-coverts comes to well below the eye (contrary to the male Blackcap) as with the Sardinian Warbler, but it is much larger than the latter. The female is browner above with a greyer head and looks rather like a large Lesser Whitethroat.
NOTES: 'Tack, tack', and a loud, rattling alarm. The song is sometimes like a Song-Thrush's or Nightingale's with short phrases and much repetition. It is a clear, mellow warble.
HABITAT: Bushes, trees, thickets, orchards, olives, gardens and mountain scrub.

GARDEN WARBLER *Sylvia borin*. Length $5\frac{1}{2}$ in. Page 132

RANGE: Only a migrant here, chiefly in spring, found from sea level to mountain regions. It breeds to the north in Europe and eastward to central Asia.
IDENTIFICATION: Brown above merging with buff beneath, without contrasts or streaks, but with rather dark legs and shortish bill.
NOTES: 'Tack, tack' and harsh churring. The song is a low, sweet, liquid, continuous warble, often of long duration, recalling the much shorter song of Blackcap.
HABITAT: Trees, bushes, gardens and especially in moist, tangled undergrowth.

BLACKCAP *Sylvia atricapilla*. Length 5½in.

RANGE: Breeds in Europe eastward to central Asia and in north-west Africa. In Lebanon it is plentiful in the river valleys, plantations and mountains at any time of the year, being a migrant and winter visitor as well as staying through the breeding season and summer in suitable habitat.

IDENTIFICATION: The male is brownish-grey above with a black cap coming down only to the top of the eye. The face, neck and underparts are pale grey. The female is slightly browner in tint with a bright chestnut cap. Immature birds have red-brown or blackish-brown caps and are tinted with buff.

NOTES: Sings from cover, usually trees or thickets, an unhurried, clear, sweet warble of pure notes. The call-notes are a short, hard 'teck, teck, teck' or harsh churring.

HABITAT: Trees, especially soft fruit trees, groves, plantations, river valleys, and the bush and scrub of the mountains, especially near water and gardens.

1. Orphean Warbler. 2. Garden Warbler. 3. Blackcap.

WHITETHROAT *Sylvia communis*. Length $5\frac{1}{2}$ in.

RANGE: A summer visitor and migrant, wintering in Africa and breeding here from sea level to the mountains, though scarce. It also breeds in Europe, a large part of Asia, and north-west Africa.
IDENTIFICATION: The male in spring and summer has a light grey head, including cheeks and ear-coverts, grey-brown upperparts with rusty or sandy edges to wing-feathers, white throat and pale pink-buff underparts. The female, young birds and autumn and winter adults of both sexes have brown or brownish heads and pale buff underparts, but are still recognized by the rusty wing margins. The feathers of the crown are often raised, giving a characteristic steep forehead and peaked crown, especially with excited males in spring song.
NOTES: The Whitethroat has a deep, harsh 'dzarr' of warning, low churring, and other sharper notes. The song is a dry, short, merry, rather hurried warble delivered in dancing song-flight, followed by a headlong dive into a bush or scrub, or it may be sung from a perch.
HABITAT: Bushes, gardens, trees and scrub from the lower areas to high mountains; also at Ammiq Swamp.

LESSER WHITETHROAT *Sylvia curruca*. Length $5\frac{1}{4}$ in.

RANGE: The breeding range of the Lesser Whitethroat covers the great bulk of central Asia westward through most of Europe. Lebanon lies towards its southern limit. It is the warbler of the Lebanon and Anti-Lebanon dry, mountain scrub, though not wholely confined to this, and it is our most plentiful mountain bird. It is a summer visitor and migrant wintering in Africa.

IDENTIFICATION: The Lesser Whitethroat is a little smaller than the Whitethroat, greyer above and whiter beneath. The head is more slate-grey in tint and the ear-coverts very dark, the legs are dark leaden, while the Whitethroat's are pale yellowish-brown. Both show white on the outer tail feathers.

NOTES: Has 'tack, tack' and 'charr' notes and a pretty little warbling song. In Europe it has a loud rattle as the most common part of the song, but this I have never heard in Lebanon.

HABITAT: Usually inside the foliage of bushes.

1. Whitethroat. 2. Lesser Whitethroat.

RÜPPELL'S WARBLER *Sylvia rüpelli.* Length $5\frac{1}{2}$ in.

RANGE: Breeds only in north-east and east Mediterranean countries and islands but in Lebanon there is no recent record of breeding. It is now probably only a rather scarce migrant.

IDENTIFICATION: The male is French-grey above, white beneath and black on the head, chin and throat, with a bold white moustache-line which divides the black of the bib from the black of the cheeks and cap. The tail is blackish with white on outer feathers. The female lacks the black and the underparts are buff-white with small blackish mottlings usually visible on the throat and head, and white moustache-stripe. The upperparts are rather more brownish-grey. Both have bright brownish-red eyes and legs.

NOTES: A loud rattling churr similar to Sardinian Warbler's, and a dry warbling and rattling song.

HABITAT: In tall, leafy ground-herbage and on the tops of low bushes and mountain scrub.

1. Rüppell's Warbler. 2. Sardinian Warbler. 3. Cyprus Warbler. 4. Ménétries Warbler.

SARDINIAN WARBLER *Sylvia melanocephala.*
Length $5\frac{1}{4}$ in.

RANGE: The breeding range is around the Mediterranean. It is a common resident in Lebanon from the foot-hills along the coast to the high mountains and Anti-Lebanon. The resident breeding birds appear to be of a paler race *S.m. momus*, but in winter the darker *S.m. melanocephala* is said to be common.
IDENTIFICATION: The male has a glossy black cap extending well down the sides of the head and nape, enclosing the eye, and a grey back; the blackish, round-ended tail shows white at the sides; throat and breast are pure white with grey at each side; eye-ring bright red. The female is grey-brown, darker on the head and the eye-ring is paler. *S.m. momus* may show a very pale rosy flush beneath, or all whitish underparts.
NOTES: The usual note is a harsh, ticking, rattling churr. The song is a dry warbling, sometimes pleasant, sometimes including a rattle, sometimes with a short song-flight.
HABITAT: Chiefly low, dry scrub, hill-side bushes and sometimes trees.

CYPRUS WARBLER *Sylvia (melanocephala) melanothorax.*

An allied form, usually treated as a separate species, but some writers consider it a race of the above, though it may be nearer *S. rüppelli.* It is resident in, and chiefly confined to Cyrpus, but a few have been recorded from Lebanon and further south in winter and early spring. It differs from the Sardinian Warbler in being darker grey above with white moustachial streak, and the throat and underparts are barred and spotted with blackish crescent markings. The female is paler with little marking beneath.

MÉNÉTRIES WARBLER *Sylvia* (*melanocephala*) *mystacea*.
Length about $5\frac{1}{4}$–$5\frac{1}{2}$ in.

RANGE: Breeds in Syria and adjoining countries eastward into Asia. In Lebanon it has been recorded and supposed breeding in times past in Anti-Lebanon, and in the Lebanon range it was definitely seen in the autumns of 1963 and 1964.
IDENTIFICATION: Like the Sardinian Warbler, it has a black head, grey back and blackish tail with white at the sides, but it shows less clear contrast between the crown and the back and is rather larger with orange-yellow rather than red eye-ring. The underparts are usually washed with pink or dull brick-red, with a pale moustache-streak, instead of being pure white, washed with grey on flanks and sides of breast or pinkish-white, as with the Sardinian. The throat and breast colour may cause confusion with Subalpine Warbler, though the Ménétries' black head is a clear distinction from the latter. Most ornithologists now consider *S. mystacea* a race of *S. melanocephala*.
NOTES: Not fully known, but a harsh, scolding 'tack, tack, tack' is usual, and the song is described as richer than the Whitethroat's, more musical and sustained, or, to the contrary, a 'weak Whitethroat-like, scratchy song' (Moor & Boswell).
HABITAT: Scrub and bushes in the hills and higher mountains, where it lurks in cover, always on the move, often scolding, very much in the manner of Sardinian Warbler.

SUBALPINE WARBLER *Sylvia cantillans*. Page 160

Uncommon migrant. Some spring records. Breeds chiefly in Mediterranean area. Male as shown on Plate 5. Female and immature birds duller with paler underparts and more brownish above. Warbling song less rapid and slightly sweeter than Sardinian Warbler's. Sometimes very short, dancing, headlong song-flight.

SPECTACLED WARBLER *Sylvia conspicillata*. Page 160

Records uncertain, may breed, probably in Anti-Lebanon. One bird in the Litani river area in early May 1967. Breeds in Jordan. More commonly breeding in western Mediterranean area. Like a very small, brighly coloured Whitethroat, usually in low cover. Yellow legs. 'Spectacles', or thin white eye-rims, are hard to see. Rather quiet, dry, warbling song, often in dancing, headlong song-flight.

Page 160

WILLOW WARBLER *Phylloscopus trochilus.* Length $4\frac{1}{4}$ in.

CHIFFCHAFF *Phylloscopus collybita.* Length $4\frac{1}{4}$ in. Page 160

RANGE: Both have a wide breeding range through central and northern Europe and Asia, that of the Chiffchaff extending to the Mediterranean in the south. Both are common on passage in spring and autumn, the Chiffchaff also being common in winter. Some olive-tinted western races, and greyer eastern races of both species occur here. A few almost pure brownish-grey and white Chiffchaffs have been seen near Ainata in September.
IDENTIFICATION: Both are greenish-olive to brownish-olive or brownish-grey above, and pale beneath tinted with yellow or pale buff to whitish. The best distinction (without wing measurements) is perhaps the colour of the legs which are usually a light yellowish-brown in the Willow Warbler and dark in the Chiffchaff, though variations overlap. The song and call-notes are the only certain guides in the field.
NOTES: The Willow Warbler's is usually of two syllables, 'hueet' or 'oo-eet' and the Chiffchaff's a single, shrill, 'wheet' or 'hweet', with some little dry scraping sounds at intervals. The Chiffchaff's quiet, scrapy-notes, however, are generally uttered at intervals in singing the usual 'chiff-chaff, chaff-chiff-chiff' sybillant song, with variations.

The Willow Warbler's song is a very sweet, liquid, lilting, descending cadence of lovely delicate tone, seldom heard in the Levant.
HABITAT: Bushes, thickets, vegetation, especially in river valleys, gardens, orchards; and the Chiffchaff also likes taller trees where available.

BONELLI'S WARBLER *Phylloscopus bonelli*. Length $4\frac{1}{2}$ in.

RANGE: The breeding range is around the Mediterranean northward to mid Europe. It appears to breed in Lebanon, and is also seen on migration to and from winter quarters in Africa.
IDENTIFICATION: Differing from other members of this genus in being rather light brownish-grey above with pale yellowish wash on the rump and under-wing and whitish on the underparts. The legs are dark. There is a pale, indistinct, buff-white, superciliary stripe.
NOTES: 'Hu-eet', like Willow Warbler's. The song is a Wood Warbler-like trill or rattle which lacks that warbler's preliminary notes and acceleration, and is somewhat more deliberate, less rapid.
HABITAT: Trees, plantations, groves, gardens, and mountain oaks and pines in the middle and lower hills.

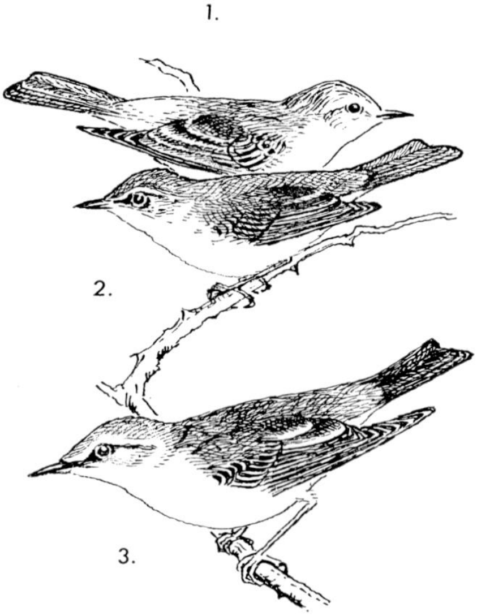

1. Bonelli's Warbler. 2. Willow Warbler (or Chiffchaff). 3. Wood Warbler.

WOOD WARBLER *Phylloscopus sibilatrix.*
Length 5 in.

RANGE: Breeds in Europe and western Asia, north of Lebanon. It is a common migrant here.
IDENTIFICATION: Larger than the preceding members of this genus, with longer wing and proportionately shorter tail. It is bright yellowish-green above with darker, brownish wings and tail, the former with yellow edges to feathers. The long supercillary-stripe, throat and upper breast are bright yellow, the belly pure white, the legs very pale, yellowish-brown.
NOTES: A soft, faint 'twit, twit, twit' and clearer, plaintive 'pew'. The song is an unmistakable stuttering 'tip-tip-tip' followed by a quickening, silvery trill. This song is interspersed with a plaintive 'pew' note.
HABITAT: Woods, trees, and on passage any leafy cover.

GREEN WARBLER *Phylloscopus nitidus.*
Length about $4\frac{1}{4}$–$4\frac{1}{2}$ in.

RANGE: Breeds from east Turkey eastward through mid Asia. One autumn record in Lebanon, by two watchers in late September 1964.
IDENTIFICATION: Bright, cold, emerald green, less yellow-green than the Wood Warbler and rather smaller and slimmer. Underparts, long superciliary-stripe and wing-bar pale yellow. The bar is often absent, or nearly so, by autumn, and the tail and wings become darker and greyer from wear. The legs are lead-grey to olive-grey, looking blackish. Plumage duller green in winter, pale beneath with some greenish-yellow or yellowish-white on the breast and a pale creamy-buff superciliary-stripe. Perhaps confusable in the field with Greenish Warbler (*P. trochiloides*) in this season (Salim Ali). Sometimes shows bright yellow on the folded wing-bend. Leg-colour should distinguish it from greener variations of Willow Warbler. No other Phylloscopus in the Near East has this 'cold' greenish hue on the upperparts: (K. Williamson).
NOTES: A clear, double note. The song is an oft-repeated strophe in the rhythm of Willow Warbler: (K. Williamson).
HABITAT: Usually juniper and scrub oak in high mountain areas.

GRACEFUL WARBLER *Prinia gracilis.*
Length $4\frac{1}{4}$–$4\frac{1}{2}$ in.

RANGE: Breeds in the Levant, south-west Asia and north-east Africa; in Lebanon it is a common bird in the coastal strip, especially of recent years when a marked increase seems to have taken place. Though resident, it seems especially abundant in spring and often swarms in vegetation and bushes near the shore, in the scrub of lower western hills, and in ruins and building sites in and around towns; its tiny, mouse-like form, long thin tail and cricket-like notes announcing its presence. Its apparent increase in spring is probably due less to numbers than to increased activity and vocal output. In autumn, when one of the two annual moults is in progress, the birds tend to be quieter and more secretive. (See Simmons in References.)
IDENTIFICATION: The Graceful Warbler is small, with a bobbing, undulating flight. It is streaked light brown above and white beneath with a very thin, long graduated tail, which forms at least half the over-all length of the tiny bird. In spring the bird is full of jerky activity with twitching wing and tail, and the male sings its monotonous, cricket-like rattle with open mouth, which, in the breeding season, is conspicuously black inside.
NOTES: Ticks and trills and rattles like a cricket.
HABITAT: In dry grass, low herbage, ruins and rubble.

FAN-TAILED WARBLER *Cisticola juncidis.* Page 142
Length 4 in.

RANGE: Breeds in Africa, around the Mediterranean and in south Asia. In Lebanon it has been seen at Ammiq Swamp a number of times, apparently breeding, and when circumstances permit, resident; and in late April 1969 seven or eight were seen in the Tapline grounds. Three of these were mounting in song.
IDENTIFICATION: A very small, dark, streaky Warbler with a short tail. It is light chestnut, heavily patterned with dark brown streaks, and pale beneath, and lacks the pale or whitish superciliary-stripe of the Sedge and Moustached Warblers. The short, round-ended, broadish tail, which is not normally fanned out, has black-and-white tips to outer feathers.
NOTES: Sings on the wing, rising and falling like a yo-yo in spring display, uttering 'chip, chip, chip', one 'chip' to each aerial bounce.
HABITAT: In marshes, fields of grain and other crops, rough grass, plains.

SPOTTED FLYCATCHER *Muscicapa striata.* Length $5\frac{1}{2}$ in.

RANGE: Breeds throughout Europe, a large part of Asia, including the Levant and in north-west Africa. In Lebanon it is a very common migrant in spring and autumn and a rather scarce summer visitor presumed breeding or attempting to, when surviving the shooting.
IDENTIFICATION: Brownish-grey with greyish-white underparts, faintly streaked on the breast, with fine dark streaks on the crown and a black bill and legs, usually seen perched in a palm or other tree, making sallies after insects flying past.
NOTES: A dry, low, chat-like 'tuck, tuck' and 'wee-tuck'; in the second version the 'wee' is a squeak followed by the dry, low, 'tuck'. The song is short, and rather feeble and squeaky.
HABITAT: Gardens, trees, outskirts of woods or thickets, creepers, etc.

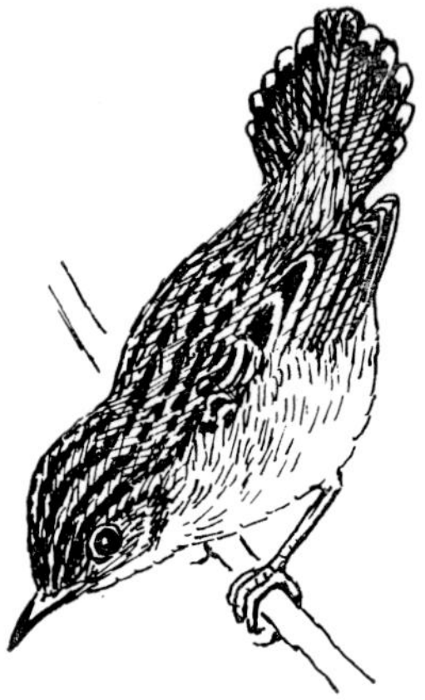

Fan-tailed Warbler.

Spotted Flycatcher.

PIED FLYCATCHER *Ficedula hypoleuca*. Length 5 in.

COLLARED FLYCATCHER *Ficedula albicollis*. Length 5 in.

RANGE: The breeding range of the Pied lies far north of Lebanon, and that of the Collared as near as south Turkey northward. Both are common on spring passage. The race *F.a. semitorquata*, which breeds in parts of the Levant, is probably confused with *F. hypoleuca*, being similar, but with more white in tail and with greyer (less brown) females.

IDENTIFICATION: The male Pied in spring is blackish or dark brownish-grey with white underparts, forehead-patch, wing-panel and sides of tail. The female, autumn male and young birds are paler with buff-white underparts and less white in wing. The male Collared Flycatcher is black with a broad collar of white, white underparts, whitish rump and large white forehead-patch. There is also more white in the wing. Female is rather greyer than Pied and shows a faint, pale collar. Autumn males are similar to females.

NOTES: A plaintive 'wheet', sharp 'wit', chat-like 'weetic, tic'. The song of the Pied is a tit-like repetition of 'chee-tit' with a twittering trill. The song of the Collared Flycatcher is a rather tit-like 'sit-sit-sit-trui-ti' and can be heard from a fair distance.

HABITAT: Woods, trees, gardens, orchards, plantations.

1 2.

1. Pied Flycatcher. 2. Collared Flycatcher.

WHINCHAT *Saxicola rubetra*. Length 5 in.

RANGE: Breeds in Europe and parts of western and central Asia. In Lebanon it is fairly common on passage.
IDENTIFICATION: The upperparts are strongly patterned with dark brown streaks with white superciliary-stripe, white wing patches and a distinctive area of white on either side of the tail. The underparts are pale cream, generally with a rosy-chestnut wash on the upper breast. The crown, ear-coverts, wings and tail are blackish brown. Females and immature birds are paler with less or no rusty wash on the breast or white on the wing. Like Stonechats they usually flick the wing, but are quieter, less hurried.
NOTES: Like Stonechat's, but has a more plaintive and persistent high note as well as a 'tic, tic', and a rather dry, warbling song.
HABITAT: Hills, uncultivated moorland, pastures, cultivation and marshes.

STONECHAT *Saxicola torquata*. Length 5 in.

RANGE: Breeds in Europe, Asia and Africa. Here it is a regular, sometimes common, winter visitor and passage migrant.
IDENTIFICATION: The male has a black head and short bib, white half-collar on each side, very dark, streaky back and wings and blackish tail. There is a white wing-bar and a white patch on the rump; the breast is rosy-chestnut. Winter birds are browner, females and young have brown heads with no white on the collar or rump. They are streaky brown above, less rosy beneath, with only mottlings of black on the throat. Stonechats constantly flick the wings and tail, often scolding or flitting low with jerky flight. They usually perch on stalks or low bushes.
NOTES: A persistent, scolding 'wee-chat, wee-chat-chat' (a sharp note followed by one or two dry, stone-clashing ones) and a very short, warbling song often in dancing song-flight.
HABITAT: As Whinchat, and especially including coastal areas.

WHEATEAR *Oenanthe oenanthe.* Length $5\frac{3}{4}$ in.

RANGE: Breeds throughout the northern part of the Old World and in Greenland and Alaska, migrating south in winter from Europe and Asia to Africa. It breeds here in the mountains and is seen on passage.
IDENTIFICATION: The male is light grey above, creamy beneath, sometimes buffish on the breast, with black ear-coverts, wings and end of tail; base of tail and rump white. The black part of the tail is T-shaped with black down the centre and across the tip, as it is with many others of this genus. Females and autumn birds have the same tail and rump pattern but are brownish above with no black.
NOTES: Like those of the Stonechat, but the 'chack, chack' note is lower and slower. The song is a pretty, varied warble with some harsher sounds and dry warbling.
HABITAT: Dry hills, mountains, and the coast.

1. Whinchat. 2. Stonechat. 3. Wheatear. 3A. Wheatear's tail.

BLACK-EARED WHEATEAR *Oenanthe hispanica.*
Length 5¾ in.

RANGE: Breeds around the Mediterranean eastward to south Iran. In Lebanon it is an abundant summer visitor and migrant, wintering in Africa.
IDENTIFICATION: The male has two phases. Perhaps the more common here is that with the black throat, chin and face, but the phase with black only on the cheeks and ear-coverts is also common. In both, the rump and tail pattern is like that of *O. oenanthe* but with slightly less black at the tip, and the scapulars, wings and under-wing are black. The underparts and back vary from nearly white with a little buff on the breast and central back to grey-brown on the back and whitish beneath with grey-buff on the breast. Females vary from sandy-buff and white to grey-brown above and are whitish beneath with buff or grey-buff breast and either whitish or dusky chin and throat. The under-wing is dusky brown.
NOTES: A high plaintive note and various, low scrapy or rasping ones which also occur in its fast, dry warbling song, while perched or circling overhead with fluttering wings.
HABITAT: Anywhere in the mountains or near the coast, including scrub, trees, bushes and wastes.

PIED WHEATEAR *Oenanthe pleschanka.* Length $5\frac{1}{2}$–$5\frac{3}{4}$ in.

RANGE: Breeds from the Black Sea eastward through Asia, with an isolated race in Cyprus, and migrates to Africa. It is not uncommon here on autumn passage.

IDENTIFICATION: The male in spring has a whitish hood and underparts and black face, throat, upper breast, central back and wings. The rump and tail are as Wheatear except that the cross-bar of the black T-shape is often narrow near the centre and widens on the outer corners, becoming almost like a W. The female is not unlike a dark female Black-eared Wheatear, being dull brown above and paler below with very dark wings above and beneath. It is duller and browner than most female Wheatears. The male in autumn has the hood obscured with brown or blackish and has a pinkish breast. (See illustration page 200.)

NOTES: Harsh low notes, variously described as 'sizzling', 'sawing', 'chack, chack', 'bizz, bizz', and like a cork being turned, with sweeter variations.

HABITAT: The coast, cliffs, mountains, rocks, stones, or bushes.

1. Pied Wheatear. 2. Black-eared Wheatear, black-throated phase. 2A. white-throated phase.

MOURNING WHEATEAR *Oenanthe lugens.*
Length about $5\frac{3}{4}$ in.

RANGE: Breeds and is chiefly resident in Palestine and North Africa eastward into south-west Asia. Its status in Lebanon is quite uncertain, but if it still occurs at all it would be in the southern part of the country.

IDENTIFICATION: The sexes are alike in the Levant-Egypt race; adult in summer has hood white, centre back black, rump and tail white with black on central tail-feathers and a narrow black band at tips of outer ones. Wing black with a large white panel on central flight feathers noticeable when flying; black face, chin and throat to sides of neck and back; underparts white with buff under tail.

This is a slightly larger, rather long-winged Wheatear, the chief diagnostic feature being the white in the wing. This shows on the upper side as a white panel crossed by black lines formed by the black outer web and shaft of each flight-feather. The under-surface of the wing is also white with a blackish tip and underwing-coverts and deep black axillaries. The bird often flutters or glides in flight, showing the white in the wing clearly.

NOTES: A short, cheerful, warbling song recalling part of the Wheatear's.

HABITAT: Rocky mountain slopes, steep ravines and arid wastes with few trees.

DESERT WHEATEAR *Oenanthe deserti.*

Length $5\frac{3}{4}$ in.

RANGE: Breeds in North Africa, north-eastward through central Asia, including Palestine and Jordan. In Lebanon it is a rare migrant or vagrant but I have seen it several times in autumn and twice in spring.

IDENTIFICATION: The Desert Wheatear is greyish-sandy or light sandy-brown above and buff beneath with a black tail, wings, face, chin and throat, and more creamy than white rump. Wing-coverts also usually show some creamy-white. The female is similar but shows little or no black on face and throat, more buff on rump, and paler wings. Sometimes in summer, she may have a mottled blackish throat.

NOTES: A plaintive, husky whistle, 'peeoo', and low, warbling 'chittachit-cheeoo'.

HABITAT: Usually plains, steppes, and semi-desert; sometimes a stony hillside.

1. Isabelline Wheatear. 2. Desert Wheatear, male, summer. 2A. female (fresh plumage). 2B. female (worn, summer plumage).

ARABIAN or FINSCH'S WHEATEAR *Oenanthe finschii.* Length about $5\frac{3}{4}$ in.

RANGE: Breeds in the Levant eastward towards central Asia. In Lebanon it is found in the mountains, though not common, apparently breeding and at least partly resident, chiefly on steep slopes and in ravines.

IDENTIFICATION: The male Finsch's Wheatear, when perched can be confused with the Mourning or Pied Wheatears, but when in flight it may be thought to be a Black-eared Wheatear because of its whitish hood and centre of back from forehead to tail. The rump and tail are as Common Wheatear. The underparts are white. The under surface of the wing shows a black lining and silvery white or pale grey on flight feathers, much paler than in the Black-eared and Pied. The black of the face, throat and upper breast is deep and wide, extending over to the scapulars and the sides of the mantle and back, with little patches of black often encroaching into the white area down the central back. Some individuals show only a narrow band of white, slightly flecked here and there with black, down the back from mantle to rump, especially in winter when some grey or brown is visible on the hood. Others are purer white both on the back and beneath. It is usually very slightly larger than the Pied with slightly longer bill. The female is light grey-brown, often showing a chestnut-brown tint on the head and ear-coverts and pale underparts. Some have the throat mottled grey to blackish. Under-wing usually pale buff as compared with brown in the females of Pied and Black-eared, and it is a paler and greyer bird generally. Juvenile is similar.

NOTES: Is said to have a short, very delicate warble, not loud. Also described as a scratchy song with clear whistles, continuous for a minute or more.

HABITAT: Stony ground and outcrops of rock in mountain ravines or on hillsides, or in open barren places. Preference for rock-rims in arid country (Bourne).

ISABELLINE WHEATEAR *Oenanthe isabellina.*
Length $6\frac{1}{2}$ in.

RANGE: Breeds chiefly in western and some parts of central Asia. In Lebanon it is not uncommon on passage even at 6,000 feet, or above. Some may still breed in lower, barren regions, but there is no recent proof, and the species is heavily shot. It winters in south-west Asia and Africa.

IDENTIFICATION: In bunches of shot birds it is easy to separate from other Wheatears at any season, by its large size alone. In the field it may also be recognized by the pale, sandy or greyish-sandy plumage of both sexes, superficially resembling the Greenland Wheatear or the females of most Wheatears, but with paler ear-coverts and facial area than these. The wings, too, are rather lighter brown than in the average females of this genus and the under-wing is nearly white, showing in the flying bird. The tail-pattern is variable but there is generally a rather wider band of brownish-black at the tip than in other Wheatears. In some, the T-shape is nearly lost and the tail appears to be largely black on the part which shows. In this respect, confusion is possible with female Desert Wheatear, though the size is different and the lower rump and tail-coverts are white (not buff and creamy-white).

NOTES: The notes vary from somewhat sparrow-like chirping and croaking to a loud whistle, sometimes recalling a goat-herd calling his flock, and a powerful, slow-tempo, varied song mimicking other birds, including larks.

HABITAT: Open country, steppes, high plateaux, plains, cultivation, open and arid mountain sides.

RUFOUS BUSH ROBIN (or RUFOUS WARBLER)

Cercotrichas galactotes. Length 6 in.

RANGE: Breeds around many parts of the Mediterranean, in Africa, Levant and Europe eastward in south Asia to central areas. Lebanon lies at the meeting point of two races, *C.g. galactotes*, the truly rufous race, which reaches southern Syria and Palestine, and *C.g. syriacus*, with grey-brown on the head and mantle, which reaches north Syria through Turkey. The race recorded in Lebanon appears to be *C.g. syriacus*, though both may occur. The species has bred in the coastal area, in the western hills and in Anti-Lebanon.
IDENTIFICATION: A lively bird with a rather long fan-shaped tail with a bold black and white border which is cocked up in the spritely manner of a wren. The upperparts of *C.g. syriacus* are grey-brown with foxy ginger rump and tail, bold, creamy superciliary-stripe and very pale brownish underparts. The slightly drooping wings and up-jerked tail are robin-like.
NOTES: The song is very sweet and pure, perhaps like part of the Skylark's and sometimes powerful. It is uttered in short phrases, from a low or high perch or in song-flight. There is a warbler-like scolding note, 'tack, tack'.
HABITAT: Bushes, plantations, groves, gardens and arid scrub, in the coastal strip, lower hills and river gorges.

ROCK THRUSH *Monticola saxatilis.* Length $7\frac{1}{2}$ in.

RANGE: Breeds in Mediterranean countries, chiefly in southern Europe and in the Levant eastward through parts of south and mid Asia. In Lebanon it is found in the mountains, though scarce. Although this is the southern border of its breeding range, it is doubtful if the species has much success here even in the highest regions owing to the shooting.
IDENTIFICATION: A rather short, sturdy bird. The male is handsome with blue head, throat, neck and upper back, white lower back, orange-chestnut lower rump and tail, blackish wings and bright orange-chestnut underparts. In winter the colours are partly hidden by buff feather-tips, and it looks more like the female which is mottled sandy-brown with crescent-markings, especially on underparts which are tinted with orange, as are the rump and tail. Young are similar.
NOTES: 'Chacking' notes. The song is varied, including a clear, pleasant warble from a perch, and a more hurried one in song-flight.
HABITAT: Found on the bare upper slopes of the mountains.

BLUE ROCK THRUSH *Monticola solitarius.* Page 176 Length 8 in.

RANGE: Breeds in Mediterranean countries and eastward right across parts of southern Asia. Here it has a strong hold and is found in river valleys just above sea level to over 6,000 feet in the mountains, breeding and at least partly resident.
IDENTIFICATION: The male is grey-blue, duller and darker on wings and tail, more dusky in winter. The female is barred in a dark-brownish-grey tone. It can be mistaken for a starling in poor light, though the shape and flight are different and the bill shorter.
NOTES: 'Chack, chack', and a thin, plaintive whistle or squeak. The short song is something like a Mistle Thrush's or perhaps a Blackbird's, but less powerful.
HABITAT: Rocky outcrops over steep ravines, rock faces or hillsides at all altitudes.

BLACK REDSTART *Phoenicurus ochruros.* Length $5\frac{1}{2}$ in.

RANGE: Breeds in Europe, Morocco and through central Asia. The race resident and breeding in the high mountains of Lebanon and Anti-Lebanon is the red-bellied, *P.o. semirufus*, restricted to Syria, Lebanon and Palestine. It descends to lower areas in winter. Birds of the European race, with grey underparts, *P.o. gibraltariensis*, pass through on passage or may appear in winter. Both are seen as late as May.

IDENTIFICATION: Robin-size, but looks slimmer. The male is a smart bird with black head, throat, breast and back and flame-red underparts, rump and tail. The female is grey with a flame-red rump and tail. The central tail-feathers of both are dark. The tail is often flickered or shuddered.

NOTES: 'Tick, tick', and a very fast, dry, scolding ticking, often with shuddering tail. The song is a rapid, shrill tinkle followed by a spluttering rattle or hiss.

HABITAT: Rocky slopes in high mountain regions, cliffs, tops of ravines, stony scrub areas above tree line, descending in winter to ruins, buildings, walls, rocks and the lower ravines.

1. Black Redstart, male (European and northern races. Lebanon race Page 65) 1A. female. 2. Redstart, male. 2A. female. 3. Robin. 4. Nightingale.

REDSTART *Phoenicurus phoenicurus*. Length $5\frac{1}{2}$ in.

RANGE: Breeds almost throughout Europe and central and north-central Asia from Turkey eastward. In Lebanon it is seen on passage in spring and autumn. The race *P.p. samamisicus* (Ehrenberg's Redstart) from the north-east has been suspected of breeding in Lebanon as there have been summer records. *P.p. phoenicurus* from the north and west, however, seems to be the more common on passage.
IDENTIFICATION: The male is distinguished from the Black Redstart by the white forehead-band and the blue-grey hood and mantle. The black of the face, chin and throat extends only to the upper breast. Lower breast and flanks are bright orange-chestnut, shading to white on abdomen and under tail. The wings and central tail feathers are brownish, the rump and most of the tail bright orange-chestnut. *P.p. samamiscus* differs only in having a white bar on the wing, the outer web of the secondaries being white edged. The female has no black on the throat and is browner or grayer with a red rump and tail. Both shiver the tail like the Black Redstart.
NOTES: Fast, ticking notes of alarm and a chat-like 'wee-tic-tic', 'weet' and 'tooeet'. The song is short, ending in a weak twitter.
HABITAT: Found in trees and bushes in the hills from the coast to about 6,000 feet.

ROBIN *Erithacus rubecula*. Length $5\frac{1}{2}$ in.

RANGE: Breeds in Europe and in a small area of North Africa eastward through parts of Asia. It winters in Lebanon and is also seen on passage to other winter quarters in North Africa.
IDENTIFICATION: Plain brown above and white beneath, with deep orange forehead, face, throat and breast. The sexes are alike, plump and spritely.
NOTES: Besides a scolding, fast, ticking and a very thin, high squeak it has a varied and beautiful song of twitters and gushes of clear notes with pauses in between. It sings nearly all the year round, even in Beirut in winter, in gardens, but in spite of this (according to Kumerloeve) many are shot.
HABITAT: Gardens, orchards, moist, rocky ravines with good cover.

NIGHTINGALE *Luscinia megarhynchos*. Length $6\frac{1}{2}$ in.

THRUSH NIGHTINGALE *Luscinia luscinia*. Length $6\frac{1}{2}$ in.

RANGE: The former breeds in Europe and parts of North Africa eastward to parts of central Asia, the southern limit reaching Lebanon. The latter ranges from eastern Europe eastward to a more northerly part of mid Asia, all lying far north of Lebanon. Here, however, they are both seen on passage, sometimes travelling in separate streams along the coast and through the Bekaa in April. Some of the former may attempt breeding but a great many are shot.
IDENTIFICATION: Both are rather like large, solid, longish, brown Robins without red breasts but with some chestnut in the tails. The Nightingale tends to have a redder tail and clear, pale underparts, the Thrush Nightingale is rather darker and more olive brown above and the pale underparts are *slightly* spotted or mottled on the breast with brown. The reddish tint at the sides of the tail may be slight and not easy to detect.
NOTES: Both have a deep, harsh warning note, a growling 'churr', a plaintive 'weet' and 'tuck, tuck', notes. Both songs are rich and powerful, with sweet, contralto warbles, and gutteral notes. The Thrush Nightingale lacks the other's unique crescendo 'pew, pew, pew', and the song tends to be more deliberate and perhaps slower and deeper, though varied.
HABITAT: Gardens, thick cover in bushes, thickets and tangled vegetation in river valleys and in the high hills.

BLUETHROAT *Luscinia svecica*. Page 160

A few records on passage. Breeds from north to mid Europe and Asia. Winters to North Africa and southern Asia, including the Levant. See on Plate 5 an intermediate phase between White-spotted and Red-spotted Bluethroats. Several phases are seen in the Levant. Spring male as shown, but one race has a red spot in the centre of the blue bib, another has a white one, and many have a spot of red and white (as shown) or other variations. Winter male has a whitish chin and sometimes black streaks and spots partly hide the blue, but birds vary greatly. Females and young birds have a whitish, black-bordered bib, with or without traces of blue and chestnut. Both sexes at all ages show a panel of chestnut-red on each side of the base of the tail.

WHITE-THROATED or PERSIAN ROBIN

Irania gutturalis. Length about $6\frac{1}{2}$–$7\frac{1}{4}$ in.

RANGE: Breeding from Asia Minor to north Palestine and eastward into central, western Asia; wintering in East Africa. In Lebanon it is scarce and secretive and though it is known to have bred here in the past and apparently still does so occasionally, the effects of so much shooting in the hills is likely to be disastrous.

IDENTIFICATION: Larger than European Robin and Redstart, often cocking or spreading the tail like a Rufous Bush Robin. The male is blue-grey on the back and rump with darker crown, white superciliary-stripe, brownish wings, tawny-chestnut under-wing-coverts and black tail. The underparts vary from orange-pink or pale buff to (more usually) bright brick-red, with white from abdomen to under tail-coverts. Black on the cheeks and ear-coverts curves down to the sides of the throat. The white on the chin and throat-centre varies in width and shape. (See page 200.) The female is brownish-grey above and on the sides of the face and neck with black tail and whitish underparts tinted buff or pale-brown on the breast, and pale chestnut on the under-wing-coverts. Some males have a black line between the white throat and tawny breast, as illustrated.

NOTES: Described as short, rich bursts, with some grating notes between. Song-flight often with fluttering wings and fanned tail and rich loud song. (See page 201.)

HABITAT: Bushes, thickets, tangled undergrowth in the mountains, and ravines.

FIELDFARE *Turdus pilaris*. Length 10 in.

RANGE: Breeds in the northern half of Asia and in northern and mid Europe. In Lebanon it is a fairly common winter visitor and migrant. The main wintering quarters are, however, in Europe and west Asia, both north of Lebanon.
IDENTIFICATION: A large, longish thrush the size of the Blackbird with a pigeon-grey head, nape and rump contrasting with dark chestnut-brown back and blackish tail and wing-tips. The underparts are white with a tawny wash on the breast and dense, bold black striations from the sides of the neck and throat to breast and flanks. In flight it shows white on the under-wing.
NOTES: A harsh 'chack' and other chattering notes. The song is a fast, thin chattering.
HABITAT: Mostly open country outside the breeding season. Recorded in the coastal strip and lower hills and (more rarely) seen in large numbers in the Bekaa.

REDWING *Turdus iliacus*. Length 8¼ in.

RANGE: Breeds in the northern half of Europe and Asia. Here it is a winter visitor, though most of the winter range lies north in west, south and central Europe and in central west Asia.
IDENTIFICATION: Smaller and shorter than the Fieldfare, not unlike the Song Thrush but rather darker above and on the cheeks, with bold cream superciliary and moustachial streaks and bright chestnut-red flanks and under-wing-coverts sometimes seen in flight. The whitish breast is more streaked than spotted with blackish striations.
NOTES: 'Chick' and 'chich-ick' and a very thin, quiet squeak, 'seees', always heard in night migration and diagnostic. Song, a short descending phrase (or sometimes rising) of four or five notes followed by a faint, jumbled warble.
HABITAT: The coastal strip, hills, and in the Bekaa in winter and on passage.

RING OUSEL *Turdus torquatus*. Page 185

A few autumn and winter records. Winter visitor from Europe or western Asia. Like Blackbird with white breast-band; paler wing has white feather-edges; pale scale-like marks on body. Female and young more grey-brown. (See illustration, page 185.)

1.

2.

3.

3A.

4.

1. Fieldfare. 2. Redwing. 3. Blackbird. 3A. female. 4. Mistle Thrush.

BLACKBIRD *Turdus merula*. Length 10 in.

RANGE: Breeds almost throughout Europe and in western and parts of southern Asia and North Africa. In Lebanon, lying on the southern fringe of the range, the Blackbird is not infrequent at all times of the year from river valleys and gardens to high mountain wadis, though always thinly distributed and scarce, especially since the increase of shooting.

IDENTIFICATION: The male is blackish or slaty-black, with orange-yellow bill and eye-rim. The female is grey-brown, paler beneath, with brown bill. The tail is fairly long and when the bird alights the tail is usually raised with deliberation, not jerked up. It is a rather quiet, shy bird, but sings in the open. On the ground it usually takes a series of long springy hops.

NOTES: A thin, wheezy 'see', warning 'chook, chook', peevish and monotonous ,'spink, spink', especially when going to roost or when excited, and a startlingly loud clucking-scream when flushed. The song is among the most beautiful and mellow to be heard, an unhurried, clear, contralto whistle in various short phrases, usually punctuated here and there with a dry, squeaky warble.

HABITAT: Gardens, bushes, thickets, orchards, groves and mountain scrub.

Plate 5

1. Cetti's Warbler.
2. Marsh Warbler.
3. Reed Warbler.
4. Savi's Warbler.
5. Subalpine Warbler, male.
6. Blackcap, male. 6A. female.
7. Spectacled Warbler.
8. Whitethroat, male, summer.
9. Wood Warbler, spring.
10. Bluethroat, male, summer. (An intermediate phase).

10A. female.
11. Willow Warbler.
12. Chiffchaff (a north-eastern race).
13. Sombre Tit.
14. Great Tit.
15. Dunnock.
16. Isabelline Wheatear.
17. Wheatear, male, summer.
18. Desert Wheatear, male.

1
2
3
4
5
6
6A
7
8
9
10
10A
11
12
13
14
15
16
17
18
S.V.BENSON

1A
2
3
1
5
4
6
7
9
8
9A
S.V. Benson
1967.

SONG THRUSH *Turdus philomelos*. Length 9 in.

RANGE: Breeds in Europe and large parts of north and central Asia. In Lebanon it is not uncommon in winter and on passage.
IDENTIFICATION: Uniform mid-brown above and spotted beneath, with yellowish-buff under-wing-coverts and a yellowish-buff wash on the breast, except with some birds from eastern regions. The breast-spots are more streaky and less large and round than the Mistle Thrush's.
NOTES: 'Chick', turning into a chattering repetition when alarmed, also scolding note of 'chink, chink' or 'tcheck, tcheck' like Blackbird's. The song is rich, sweet and clear in short, varied phrases often repeated.
HABITAT: Seen in the river valleys and hills, also in the Bekaa, usually in trees, gardens, and mountain scrub. Many are shot in or near town gardens, plantations and groves.

MISTLE THRUSH *Turdus viscivorus*. Length 10½ in. Page 159

RANGE: Breeds in a great part of central and northern Asia as far south as Lebanon, and almost throughout Europe, also in part of North Africa. Here it is fairly common in winter and on passage. Great numbers are shot, and though it may attempt breeding now and then, it is doubtful if it ever succeeds.
IDENTIFICATION: Much larger, greyer and whiter than Song Thrush. The upperparts are light grey-brown. The underparts whitish with roundish black spots, larger than Song Thrush's, and the underside of the wing shows very white in flight. The outer tail-feathers have white tips.
NOTES: Makes a loud, strident churring and a thin 'seep' like the Redwing's. The song is a short, loud phrase usually shouted from the top of a tree or other exposed place and superficially not unlike the Blackbird's, though less musical than those of some other members of this family.
HABITAT: River valleys and woods in the mountains and coastal strip, and right up to the old Cedars at 6,000 feet.

Plate 6

1. Mourning Wheatear, with 1A. spread wing.
2. Black-eared Wheatear, male, black-throated phase.
3. Finsch's Wheatear, male and female.
4. Palestine Sunbird, male and female.
5. Olivaceous Warbler.
6. Upcher's Warbler.
7. Graceful Warbler.
8. Bulbul.
9. White-throated Robin, male and female, 9A. head of male, usual type.

SOMBRE TIT *Parus lugubris*. Length $5\frac{1}{2}$ in.

RANGE: Breeds from the Balkans and Asia Minor eastward through Persia. Its breeding records in Lebanon are of particular interest, as the nearest accepted breeding area is in Turkey. It is, however, probable that it has bred in Lebanon since early in the last century, as it has been recorded from time to time in suitable places. Since 1956 two or three pairs have been seen almost annually in one of these places, and at least one of the pairs was feeding young each year, according to our records.
IDENTIFICATION: A large Tit, the size of the Great Tit, with a big head and fairly stout bill, greyish-brown with pale underparts, brownish-black cap and bib (browner in female) and a wide white or whitish patch across cheeks and ear-coverts to sides of neck.
NOTES: A low, dry 'chirruf' or 'chirerer' and harsh 'chaar'; also sometimes some soft little squeaks or churring.
HABITAT: Rocky and scrubby hills, cedars, pines and other wooded places.

1. Sombre Tit. 2. Great Tit. 3. Coal Tit. 4. Blue Tit.

GREAT TIT *Parus major*. Length $5\frac{1}{2}$ in.

RANGE: One of the most abundant and successful resident breeding birds in Lebanon, and also in Europe and Asia and in north-west Africa.
IDENTIFICATION: A large Tit with greenish-grey mantle, blue-grey wings, rump and tail and a whitish wing-bar. The underparts are pale yellow with a black band down the centre which joins the black bib. The head and sides of neck are also black and the cheeks and ear-coverts pure white.
NOTES: A metallic 'chink', thin 'Si-si-si', scolding 'tsee-char-char' and churring. Song, 'teacher, teacher', oft repeated, the first syllable being high and sharp.
HABITAT: River valleys with trees or bushes, gardens, orchards, plantations, groves, and pines chiefly in the lower hills but in some places up to nearly 6,000 feet.

COAL TIT *Parus ater*. Length $4\frac{1}{2}$ in.

RANGE: Breeds in Europe and Asia and in parts of North Africa, but is only found in isolated areas in southern Asia. It breeds here and in Cyprus in suitable trees in the hills.
IDENTIFICATION: Small with grey or slightly olive-grey upperparts with a double white bar on the wing and whitish underparts with a little grey or grey-buff on the flanks. The head is black with a large white patch on the nape. The cheeks and ear-coverts are whitish, the chin and throat black.
NOTES: Scolding 'chee-chee-chee', thin, squeaky 'si-si-si', diagnostic, clear, plaintive 'su-ee', and song like Great Tit's but sweeter, clearer, less loud, more varied.
HABITAT: Pines and cedars in the mountains.

BLUE TIT *Parus caeruleus*. Length $4\frac{1}{2}$ in.

An occasional winter visitor from surrounding countries. Several seen in coastal river valleys and trees during the last decade. Head blue and white, wings and tail blue, back greenish, underparts yellow.

NEUMAYER'S ROCK NUTHATCH *Sitta neumayer.* Length $5\frac{1}{2}$ in.

RANGE: Breeds from the Balkans and Levant east to Persia. In Lebanon it is a not uncommon resident breeding in the mountains.
IDENTIFICATION: A short, rather stout, light blue-grey bird with a rather long and powerful bill and flat-topped head. The underparts are whitish with slight brownish wash on the flanks. The bill is dark and a blackish band runs from it, through the eye, to behind the ear-coverts. This bird has a rather tit-like way of creeping about and clinging to perpendicular surfaces head downward or any way up.
NOTES: 'Whit, whit', and a staccato trill, accelerating and slowing down again, loud, ringing and shrill.
HABITAT: Rocky ravines and gorges, cliffs and steep mountains. Makes a mud entrance-passage to nest in rock crevice, often under an overhang.

WALL CREEPER *Tichodroma muraria*. Length 6½ in.

RANGE: Breeds in the mountains of southern Europe and parts of southern Asia. In Lebanon it is found in the mountains, though rather scarce, and may be breeding and resident there.
IDENTIFICATION: A striking bird with butterfly-shaped crimson wings with wide black fringes and two rows of large white spots on the blackish primaries. In summer the throat and breast are black, in winter they are whitish. The head and mantle and the rest of the underparts are grey, the short, square tail black with a grey tip and large white spots on the ends of the outer tail feathers. From underneath, the rounded wings look blackish with two rows of large white spots and with pinkish-crimson showing at the base only. The bill is long, thin and slightly down-curved. The bird's behaviour attracts the eye as it creeps up a sheer face of rock in upward jerks, flicking the wings half open at each jerk and displaying the crimson parts.
NOTES: A high, thin, clear cascade of little piping notes, and a song of louder, sweeter notes.
HABITAT: Mountain precipices, narrow ravines, sheer rock-walls.

PALESTINE SUNBIRD *Nectarinia osea.* Length about $4\frac{1}{4}$ in.

RANGE: Breeds from southern Syria and Lebanon south to Jordan and Palestine, and probably in Arabia and in parts of Africa. In Lebanon its breeding is limited to a very few places in the southern part where protection has been afforded, also a breeding record in Beirut and a party of five in the Latani river valley in April, but, normally, it is only a winter visitor penetrating at least as far north as Beirut.

IDENTIFICATION: Male in breeding plumage, which is gained during the winter and lost in late summer, iridescent, metallic green and peacock-blue with violet breast and forehead, blue chin and black abdomen, with an orange and yellow tuft each side of the breast. The female is darkish grey-brown above and very pale brown beneath with a very dark tail. Male in autumn is more like female but with blackish wings and tail, metallic green wing-coverts and a few metallic tips here and there on the body. Both are very tiny, delicate-looking birds with down-curved bills of fair length, but not as long as those of many other Sunbirds. Without the bill the bird would be only $3\frac{1}{2}$ inches long.

NOTES: P. A. D. Hollom records many Tit-like notes and some like Warblers'; flight note, 'tzik-tzik', sometimes running into a trill.

HABITAT: Chiefly low country with gardens, orchards, flowers and flowering shrubs, tangled bushes and creepers along river banks, lanes, etc.

HOUSE SPARROW *Passer domesticus*. Length 5¾ in.

RANGE: Breeds in Europe and most parts of Asia, and in North Africa and Nile region, as well as in other parts of the world. In Lebanon a rather pale race is as common as the species is everywhere else.
IDENTIFICATION: The male has a dark brownish head with dark grey cap and off-white cheeks and underparts, and a black bib, streaky brown back and wings with narrow whitish wing-bars, brownish-grey rump and brown tail. The female lacks the bib and head pattern and is streaky brown with pale underparts.
NOTES: Chirping, churring and higher cheeping notes.
HABITAT: Prefers towns, villages and cultivation, nesting chiefly in buildings.

SPANISH SPARROW *Passer hispaniolensis*. Length 5¾ in.

Page 168

RANGE: Restricted to Mediterranean countries and part of southern mid-Asia east to Turkestan. In Lebanon it is a migrant, seen chiefly in spring, and it also breeds in a few places offering suitable habitat. In recent years there was a breeding colony by the Nahr-el-Kelb, but in 1962 a group of large trees by a Café and the river was pollarded or cut down and the colony was lost.
IDENTIFICATION: The male has a chestnut-brown head with white cheeks, and the large black bib joins heavy black streaks on the flanks and over the 'shoulders' to upper back. Wings have short whitish bars. Female, like other hen sparrows, but with faint streaks on flanks, streaky back and whiter cheeks.
NOTES: Like House Sparrow's but louder and clearer in chorus.
HABITAT: Found in trees and bushes, usually nesting in colonies with globular nests in trees, and sometimes in the base of a big stick nest of a large bird.

1.

2.

1. House Sparrow, male and female. 2. Spanish Sparrow, male and female.

ROCK SPARROW *Petronia petronia*. Length 5½ in.

RANGE: Breeds in Mediterranean countries eastward through Asia in suitable areas. In Lebanon it is resident and common in all the higher arid regions, and is said to breed also in ruins in the Bekaa. It is most conspicuous in the large autumn flocks which gather in the Cedars area and at other rocky places at high altitudes.
IDENTIFICATION: In flight it might be mistaken for a very pale female House Sparrow, were it not for squeaky notes and large white spots on the tail tip. At close range it is seen to have wide pale and dark stripes on the sides of the pale crown, on the upper back, and faintly beneath, and the much more sandy lower back and rump are noticeable in flight. A yellow patch on the throat is seldom discernable, but the thick, palish bill is.
NOTES: Wheezy and shrill double call notes sound like a constant, querulous 'cheese' or 'chee-se'; also lower, sparrow-like chirps.
HABITAT: Rocky hills and mountains, ravines, cliffs and ruins.

PLOCEIDAE Page 177

PALE ROCK SPARROW *Petronia brachydactyla.*
Length $5\frac{1}{4}$–$5\frac{1}{2}$ in.

RANGE: Breeds from Lebanon and Syria eastward to Khorasan and Transcaspia. It is only recorded as breeding in Anti-Lebanon here, but I have seen it in little flocks in the Lebanon range in autumn; whisp after whisp of birds on the move for two days.
IDENTIFICATION: A little smaller and slimmer than the Rock Sparrow, unstriped, with no yellow on the throat, no white spots on central tail-feathers and rather smaller ones on the tips of the outer feathers.
NOTES: The spring song, sung from the top of a rock or perched on a stone, is a wheezy, trilling 'tee-zeeeeze' or 'tee-tee-cheeeese' recalling the second half of a Yellowhammer's song ('. . . and no cheese') or the song of some other Bunting, or like the drawling wheeze of the Greenfinch or the dry tinkle of the Corn Bunting. Flight note heard from pairs in chasing courtship, a low, soft, purring trill or churr. 'A close flock of about thirty, the song and chorus being a grasshopper-like "zing-ling zeee" or "zwee" ' (Hollom). 'Perches rather upright and wheezes in a manner resembling the drawl of the Greenfinch . . . "tee-zee" . . . It also has a sharp "twee-ou" call . . . The call is a distinctive field-character. Found in lonely nullahs . . . low hills of loose sand' (Moor and Boswell).
HABITAT: Desolate stony slopes and rocky areas above ravines at moderate altitudes.

Family FRINGILLIDAE Page 176

BRAMBLING *Fringilla montifringilla.*

Only two or three winter records. Northern species. Seen here only in winter when it looks rather like a Chaffinch, but the male's head is darker than the latters, including the cheeks, and both sexes have white rumps shown clearly in flight (not greenish rumps as with Chaffinch). Summer male has black head and upper back.

CHAFFINCH *Fringilla coelebs*. Length 6 in.

RANGE: Breeds throughout Europe eastward to mid Asia, in North Africa and the Levant. In Lebanon it breeds in the high mountains in cedar and pine forest in mid to north Lebanon, and also in some lower areas, in other trees, chiefly orchards. It is also a migrant and winter visitor in suitable habitat.

IDENTIFICATION: The slate-blue head and pink-buff face and breast of the male are distinctive, also, in flight, the bold white patch and bar on the wing and the white on outer tail-feathers. Both sexes have these white markings though the female's bars are rather less conspicuous and she is light brown, paler beneath. The male is chestnut-brown on the mantle and greenish on the rump.

NOTES: A ringing 'quink' or 'spink', a plaintive, Willow-Warbler-like 'wheet', a quiet 'sup' in flight and a low wheezing 'sweeee' like the Greenfinch's, often called the 'rain call'. The song is a rollicking cadence, short and loud. Said very fast, it has been rendered by W. Garstang as 'Chip chip chip tell tell tell cherry-erry-erry tissi cheweeo'.

HABITAT: As above.

female male

Page 177

TRISTRAM'S or SYRIAN SERIN *Serinus syriacus*. Length 4¾ in.

RANGE: Breeds in Lebanon, Syria and Jordan in the mountains. In winter it is found in lower areas and also in Iraq and Palestine.
IDENTIFICATION: Much less streaked than Serin and has a very pale grey-brown wash on the yellow breast and throat and on the green and yellow back. Rump paler yellow. In general, a duller version of the Serin. The forehead is clear bright yellow. Autumn flocks of young birds may have no yellow on rumps or elsewhere.
NOTES: A low, husky, trilling or twittering note and a pretty little twittering song, faster and briefer than Linnet's.
HABITAT: Chiefly in mountain scrub and mountain vegetation, often in arid areas. Also in the Bekaa, especially in winter.

SERIN *Serinus serinus*. Length 4½ in. Pages 174, 176

RANGE: Breeds in continental Europe, western North Africa and Asia Minor. In Lebanon it is a winter visitor, lingering into spring, chiefly along the coastal strip.
IDENTIFICATION: A very small, yellowish, short-billed finch with short, dark, forked tail, greenish-brown back and wings, bright lemon-yellow forehead, breast and rump with clear-cut dark streaks on sides of breast, flanks and upperparts. The female is much duller with more streaks on the breast, but she also has a yellow rump showing in flight. Winter males are less yellow and young birds in autumn lack even the yellow rump.
NOTES: A thin, high twittering or chattering flight-note and a Goldfinch-like plaintive 'sueet'. The song, which is often sung on the wing in fluttering or gliding flight, is a sibilant, rapid twittering, with occasional trills. At times it has a Corn Bunting sound, aptly described as 'sizzling' by P. A. D. Hollom.
HABITAT: Chiefly at low levels, especially in coastal areas, orchards, groves, trees, river valleys.

Page 177

GOLD-FRONTED or RED-FRONTED SERIN

Serinus pusillus. Length about $4\frac{1}{2}$ in.

RANGE: Breeds in Asia Minor eastward through western and south-central Asia. In winter, though largely resident, it wanders down into the mountains of the Levant. Tristram stated that it occurred in Lebanon, Van Dyck collected four skins. Kumerloeve suggests that it may possibly breed in the Syrian and Lebanon ranges, but the best chance of finding it here is on its autumn or early winter wanderings in the high parts of the Lebanon range where I saw a party of seven in immature and autumn plumage.

IDENTIFICATION: About the size and shape of other Serins. The male in summer has a dark chestnut-brown head and throat (sometimes looking black) and a large fiery-orange forehead-patch. The rest of the plumage above is streaked grey-brown with paler edges to wing-coverts and a little pale buff and yellow on the rump. Underparts are whitish with buff and dark streaks. Flight feathers and tail are dark with pale edges. The female has a paler chestnut-tinted head with no flame-coloured forehead-patch, and has a generally streaky grey-brown appearance with slightly paler rump, and with cinnamon-buff on the wing-coverts. Family parties, such as might be seen here in autumn or winter, are mottled and streaked by pale feather-margins and the slate-grey wing-coverts are widely edged with pale buff. The flight feathers and tail are blackish with pale edges. Some males at this season have a little yellow on the rump and both sexes show some pale chestnut-brown with dark streaks on the head and a faint chestnut wash on the throat, but with no orange forehead-patch. Bill and legs are black.

NOTES: Twittering or trilling flight-notes recalling Syrian Serin. The song is a squeaky warble which sounded to me like 'ch-wichy-weasel' repeated several times.

HABITAT: High mountain ranges, often above tree-level.

SISKIN *Carduelis spinus.*

Page 185

Rarely recorded here in winter, but kept as cage-bird. Species from northern Europe and Asia. Serin size. Yellow rump and breast, yellow and black tail and wings, greenish back; male, black crown and chin.

GREENFINCH *Carduelis chloris*. Length $5\frac{3}{4}$ in.

RANGE: Breeds almost throughout Europe and western Asia, also in North Africa. In Lebanon it is common, especially in the hills. It is resident and also a winter visitor, breeding where circumstances permit.

IDENTIFICATION: A stout yellowish-olive-green bird with bright yellow at the sides of the forked tail and edges of primaries, yellowish-green rump, and rather, thick, pale bill. Female and immature birds are duller, greyer or browner.

NOTES: A nasal, resonant 'su-ee', a low 'chu, chu', long-drawn 'zweee', and twittering, also song consisting of these variations and a pea-like rattle or trill as follows: 'trrrrr, chu-chu-chu, zweeee, chu-chu-chu', ending in a rattling twitter, but with pauses and variations. Song is from a perch or in gliding song-flight with raised wings and slow-motion wing-beat.

HABITAT: Chiefly in the hills at heights of up to or over 6,000 feet, in pines, cedars, and small trees and bushes. Also common in orchards, plantations and gardens at sea level, especially outside the breeding season.

Serin.

Greenfinch.

GOLDFINCH *Carduelis carduelis*. Length $4\frac{3}{4}$ in.

RANGE: Breeds in Europe, North Africa and mid to west Asia. In Lebanon it is not only a favourite cage bird, but a resident breeding bird in the hills and a winter visitor.
IDENTIFICATION: Easily recognized in flight by bold wing-pattern of black with a very wide band of bright yellow along the full wing-length, a white rump and black and white tail. The chin, forehead and face are bright red, the sides of the head and ear-coverts to throat are white framed by a wide black band from crown to sides of neck. The mantle is greyish-buff, breast and flanks washed with the same tint; white spots on tips of flight-feathers; forked tail; pale, creamy, sharp bill. Immature birds in autumn have grey-buff heads like the mantle and breast, but wings as adult. Seen flying in ones or twos or in dancing, undulating, twittering small flocks.
NOTES: Tinkling flight-notes or contact-notes, 'swit-swit-a-wit', and a gentle, plaintive, nasal 'tsu-ee' and song of similar tinkling, canary-like notes.
HABITAT: Chiefly in the hills and mountains, especially where water is available, and in winter chiefly at lower altitudes, near trees and bushes, orchards, plantations, groves, gardens.

LINNET *Acanthis cannabina.* Length $5\frac{1}{4}$ in.

RANGE: Breeds in Europe and in western to parts of mid Asia and in North Africa. In Lebanon it is resident, breeding in the high mountains, and a winter visitor at lower levels as well as high up.
IDENTIFICATION: The male in spring and summer has pale grey on the head and nape, with deep rosy-pink to crimson on the breast and forehead, light chestnut-brown mantle, and whitish underparts. The female lacks pink or red and is streaked. In both, the darkish wing and tail-feathers are narrowly edged with white. Immature birds are browner and more streaked. All have forked tails. In winter all are slightly browner and duller and without any red.
NOTES: A constant, liquid, staccato twitter in flight. Song is of varied, sweet, unhurried notes and twitters, and occasionally staccato trills with many pauses. Females also sing, but have only a few short phrases.
HABITAT: Open, often arid country in the high mountains with scrub, and in winter also near cultivation.

Plate 7

1. Brambling, male, autumn.
2. Hawfinch, male.
3. Greenfinch, male, summer.
4. Serin, male, spring.
5. Black-headed Bunting, male, summer.
6. Cretzschmar's Bunting, male, summer.
7. Rock Bunting, male, summer.
8. Chaffinch, male, summer.
9. Goldfinch.
10. Linnet, male, summer.
11. Nightingale.
12. Crested Lark.
13. Grey Wagtail, male (black throat-patch summer).
14. Yellow Wagtail (Blue headed), male, spring.
15. Rock Thrush, male, summer.
16. Blue Rock Thrush, male, summer, and female.
17. Tawny Pipit.
18. Long-billed Pipit.

1
2
3
4
5
6
7
8
9
10
11
12
13
14
15
16
17
18
1968

A
I
B
IC
2
3
A
B
4
A
B
5
B
6
A
S.V. Benson 1966
6C
ID
5C
SECONDARY-COVERT
SECONDARY
OUTER WEB SHOWING PINK
INNER WEB SHOWING WHITE

CRIMSON-WINGED FINCH *Rhodopechys sanguinea.* Length about 6 in.

RANGE: Breeds in the Atlas mountains and in the Levant eastward to Afghanistan and Turkestan. In Lebanon it is breeding in the high mountains and is sometimes seen in rather large numbers on the heights in local autumn movements comprising many small straggling flocks.

IDENTIFICATION: A stout, thickset finch with heavy, rather pale, brownish or yellowish bill, and with mottled sandy-brown plumage above and on the breast and flanks, with dark or black crown and white on the belly. The flight-feathers and tail are partly black with wide, deep pink outer edges to the former, and bold white edges to most of the latter and to the tips of the secondaries. Most wing-coverts show deep pink, the primary-coverts black-tipped, and there are wider areas of pink on inner secondaries. In flight a long panel of pink or pinkish-silver and white shows on the wing, with black fringes, as an area of white on the inner webs is momentarily revealed. Note the drawing of a secondary feather opposite. Part of this white area is revealed at full wing-stretch, but the half open wing looks largely pink. Adult males have some pink on the sides of the face and bright pink on the rump and at the edges of the tail-feathers near the base, and mottled black on the crown and nape. Autumn flocks contain many birds with less pink on the wing and none on the rump, but with whitish tips to upper tail-coverts.

NOTES: It has a silvery twitter in flight and some pleasant, lark-like notes and various lower ones. 'Called "tlweep" on flushing or when fluttering up from the ground to move a few yards, the note rich, musical and fluty, louder than Woodlark but with some of its quality; and in flight overhead a more rippling "turdel-edel-weep-ou". A male working over the ground gave an occasional "whee-tell-ee" or "whee-tell-eer", musical and rather quiet' (Hollom).

HABITAT: Chiefly dry mountain regions and deserts, also among bushes and scrub.

Plate 8

1. Desert Finch, adults spring, 1A. female. 1B. male. 1C. immature.
1D. Partly spread wing.
2. Pale Rock Sparrow.
3. Red-fronted Serin, autumn-winter.
4. Tristram's Serin, 4A. male. 4B. female.
5. Trumpeter Finch. 5A. spring male. 5B. female. 5C. partly spread wing.
6. Crimson-winged Finch. 6A. male. 6B. female. 6C. partly spread wing and secondary wing-feather.

DESERT FINCH *Rhodopechys obsoleta*. Length about $5\frac{1}{2}$ in.

RANGE: It is said to breed in Palestine and Syria eastward to parts of mid-Asia, and was recorded as a winter visitor to Lebanon by Aharoni. It has also been present in autumn movements on at least one recent occasion when a number were heard and seen in flight and others perched on rocks. The flight-note is remarkable.

IDENTIFICATION: Smaller than *R. sanguinea*, with no pink on the rump and with very smooth, unstreaked, unmottled, pale, sandy-greyish upperparts shading to pale chestnut on the rump, and even paler underparts with white on the abdomen. The plumage varies according to age, seasons and sex, and tail-feathers are black with wide white borders, or dark brown with pale edges. The tail is deeply forked as with the Goldfinch. The primaries are black with broad white edges and white on the inner web. The secondaries are the same but have pale rose-pink outer webs. It differs from *R. sanguinea* in flight in showing no pink on the primaries, only black and white. The primary coverts show pink with black-and-white tips. The very stout, conical bill is also variable, but is usually black or grey-black in the breeding season with rusty-blackish lores in the male. At other times the bill is not so dark, often quite pale, brownish or dark red-brown. Females bills tend to be browner. Young birds in autumn may have pale, straw-colour bills, tinted orange on the upper mandible, but by the spring these are black with yellow patches. Distinctions between these out of season birds and the Trumpeter Finch are not so obvious as might be imagined. When the former are perched, the rose pink and most of the white in the wing can be hidden in the thick cushions of scapulars and flank feathers, and the bill, which is the easiest field mark when blackish, is sometimes not far from the shade of the Trumpeter Finch's. However, the Desert Finch always has a more pale-biscuit shade of head and body. It perches rather upright, sometimes elongating the plump body and craning the thick neck at the observer. The dark, beady eye is characteristic.

NOTES: A high, tinkling or twittering trill, rising and falling in tone, illusive, heard from birds on the wing. It appears to be used as a flight-note and contact note. 'The note was a strange ventriloqual, high-pitched trill, easy to overlook but of considerable carrying power' (Bourne). 'When a flock of 60 to 70 birds was disturbed in the desert, they flew off with much twittering . . . a metallic twitter, "Tr-r-r-r" ' (Chapman). 'March . . . one singing and preening at the same time, so perhaps more sub-song than typical, full song . . . a very slow tempo, somewhat Linnet-like song going on and on'

(Hollom). 'The most pronounced field-character is the call, a rippling "r-r-r-r-r-ee" which descends in pitch and rises . . . uttered in flight' (Moor and Boswell).
HABITAT: Plateaux, deserts, hills, gardens, bushes and often near trees.

TRUMPETER FINCH *Rhodopechys githaginea.* Page 177

Length about $5\frac{1}{4}$ in.

RANGE: Breeds in Africa and south-west Asia including Palestine, Jordan and Lebanon. Here the breeding records are very scarce and only in Anti-Lebanon, but some birds have been seen on the bare heights of the Lebanon mountains in autumn.
IDENTIFICATION: This is the smallest of the three *Rhodopechys* finches of this part of the world, and the plumage is unstreaked greyish-brown above, greyest on the head, and very pale beneath with a rosy wash (sometimes very slight or absent in females and winter males) on the underparts, rump and wings. The wings and tail are dusky, nearly black towards the ends, some feathers narrowly edged with red, some with pale or inconspicuous whitish edges. Young birds are more buff, females slightly more brown in tone. The bill is stout and deep orange to coral-red in spring males; in females and autumn males it is orange-brown, pale orange or yellowish-horn.
NOTES: A strange, buzzing, vibrant call like a feeble tin trumpet, variously described as 'a nasal, bleeting note—like the distant sound of a child's toy trumpet' (Mountfort) or as a 'buzzing note' or like 'a very small puncture under water' (Moor and Boswell).
HABITAT: Dry mountain regions and deserts.

HAWFINCH *Coccothraustes coccothraustes.* Page 176

Rarely recorded in winter. Wide breeding range in Europe and Asia. Male as shown. Female a little paler, immature with yellowish (not black) throat-patch, and barring, especially on underparts.

CORN BUNTING *Emberiza calandra*. Length 7 in.

RANGE: Breeds in Europe eastward to parts of southern mid-Asia, also in North Africa. In Lebanon it is resident, breeding where possible, but apparently rather badly shot-up. It is also fairly common in suitable areas in winter.
IDENTIFICATION: A stout, large, heavy-looking straw-coloured or pale-brown bunting with dark striations above and beneath, forked tail and thick bill. There is no white in tail or wings and very little contrast. Easily identified by jingling song.
NOTES: Usual notes, a dry, crisp 'wit' or 'wit-a-wit', or a twitter, sometimes a wheezy 'zeep'. The song is an unmistakable high, squeaky, jingling rattle like the shaking of a bunch of little keys or the shattering and falling of thin glass. The bird sings persistently nearly all the year round.
HABITAT: Open country, often with cultivation, on east and west slopes of the Lebanon range and in the Bekaa.

CINEREOUS BUNTING *Emberiza cineracea.*
Length about $6\frac{1}{2}$ in.

Often called (somewhat misleadingly) 'Ashy-headed Bunting.' Here it is an uncommon migrant in spring and autumn. Probably the race *E.c. semenowi* (breeding in south-western India and perhaps Syria), with lemon-yellow throat and abdomen, dull greenish-yellow head, tinted brown; greyish breast band; grey-brown, dark-streaked back, and brown tail with some white on outer feathers, has been seen in Lebanon; or else the race which breeds in Aegean and Turkey south-eastwards, with dull yellow head, yellow throat, but with little or no yellow beneath and more grey in general, with white belly, may pass through occasionally on passage. Females and immature birds browner, more streaky.

Both races winter southward.

HABITAT: Arid, stony or rocky mountain slopes.

YELLOWHAMMER *Emberiza citrinella.* Page 185

A few winter records. Breeds in Europe and Asia, wintering south to Levant. Yellow head and underparts, striped brown back, rusty rump, white in tail. Much brighter colours than with Cinereous Bunting. Female and young more streaked brown.

Cinereous Bunting.

ROCK BUNTING *Emberiza cia*. Length 6¼ in.

RANGE: Breeds mostly in southern Europe and Mediterranean countries, including North Africa and the Levant, eastward right through south mid-Asia in suitable areas. In Lebanon it appears to be not uncommon but a thinly scattered resident, breeding in the high mountain regions, often flocking and plentiful in autumnal (probably local) movements.
IDENTIFICATION: A typical bunting, having longish tail, chestnut back and rump, streaked on upper back, dark wings and tail with conspicuous white on outer tail-feathers. The head and upper breast are pale grey with narrow black bands above the eye, through the eye and framing the cheek and ear-coverts. Below the pale-grey upper breast the underparts are light chestnut. The female is similar but less clearly marked and brightly coloured, and rather more streaked. Young in autumn flocks are streaky brown and recognized chiefly by chestnut-buff on underparts, and adults in autumn are also slightly duller in colour.
NOTES: A thin, high 'sip' or sometimes a bubbling twitter. Song is short and feeble; a cross between Yellowhammer's and Reed Bunting's, rather high and shrill, with rising last note.
HABITAT: Around low scrub and mountain plants mostly in rocky, high mountains, but sometimes at lower altitudes, especially in winter.

 Page 184

ORTOLAN BUNTING *Emberiza hortulana*. Length $6\frac{1}{2}$ in.

RANGE: Breeds in Europe eastward to central Asia, including the Levant. In Lebanon it is a passage migrant, often in large numbers in autumn when many hundreds are shot and displayed in bunches. It has bred in small numbers in the hills, and if it still succeeds in breeding at all, is found at 5,000 or 6,000 feet.
IDENTIFICATION: Both Ortolan and Cretzschmar's Buntings have streaked chestnut-brown upperparts, white on outer tail-feathers and a deep rusty wash on the underparts, as with Rock Bunting. The Ortolan has the head and breast green-grey with lemon-yellow throat and moustachial stripe (rather duller in autumn). The female is paler and duller but is distinguished from female Cretzschmar's by some yellow on the throat. Young are streaky brown, but at all ages both sexes show coral-pink bill and pale yellow eye rims, as with Cretzschmar's.
NOTES: A high 'seep', clear 'seeu' and other short notes; varied song of limited scope and tone, chiefly 'zeu-zeu-zeu-see-see' or this in reverse (slower and lower-pitched than Yellowhammer's), and with other, more pleasing notes sometimes introduced.
HABITAT: Hilly country with bushes and scrub, also cultivation.

CRETZSCHMAR'S BUNTING *Emberiza caesia*. Page 176 Length $6\frac{1}{4}$ in.

RANGE: Breeds in the east Mediterranean area including Greece, Turkey, Syria and Lebanon, and probably Jordan and Palestine. Not uncommon in the breeding season in the lower mountain ranges in luxuriant bushy places, up to 4,000 or 5,000 feet. It is also a common migrant and many are shot.
IDENTIFICATION: Distinguished from Ortolan by very blue-grey head and breast with rusty orange-yellow throat and moustachial stripe and darker rusty underparts. Females and autumn males are rather duller, and young are brown and streaky, but at all ages, both sexes show a pinkish bill and narrow, pale yellow eye-rim.
NOTES: Like Ortolan's but harsher; song also similar but very short.
HABITAT: As Ortolan's, but also in arid regions of rocks and dry, small scrub.

BLACK-HEADED BUNTING *Emberiza melanocephala.* Length 6½ in.

RANGE: Breeds in south-east Europe east to the Levant and to mid Asia. In Lebanon it is a summer visitor, breeding with more or less success in the hills and mountains and in open country in north Lebanon in spite of cruel persecution from shooters.
IDENTIFICATION: The male is a handsome bunting with bright yellow underparts, chestnut-brown upperparts and black head with yellow half-collar on sides of neck. Female is brown with yellowish underparts and no black. Neither have white outer tail-feathers. Autumn males are duller and browner; young birds in autumn brownish-buff beneath with yellow on under tail-coverts.
NOTES: A sharp 'sit' and a lower, nasal note. The song is a pleasant, rapid, musical tinkle or warble, prefaced by hesitant 'zit-zit' notes.
HABITAT: Open country with bushes, reeds, small, sparse trees and sometimes cultivation, also hills and mountains with scrub or bushes.

Ortolan Bunting.

Black-headed Bunting.

REED BUNTING *Emberiza schoeniclus.*

At least one in Ammiq Swamp, May 1965. One male giving snatches of song. Breeds as near as Syria. Black head and bib; white moustache-stripe, neck, and underparts; striped brown back and wings, white outer tail-feathers. Female and autumn birds, browner, boldly streaked, whitish and blackish moustache-stripes.

LITTLE BUNTING *Emberiza pusilla.*

One record. Breeds in Asia and north-east Europe, wintering south and eastward. Small Bunting, size of Twite or Linnet. Streaked, brown. Male has rusty head marked with black only in breeding season. Female less rusty on crown and cheeks.

SPECIES OCCASIONALLY RECORDED

1. Reed Bunting. 2. Yellowhammer. (page 181)
3. Siskin. (page 173) 4. Ring Ousel. (page 158)

ADDITIONAL SPECIES RECORDED IN LEBANON OR NEAR BY

Family PODICIPEDIDAE

BLACK-NECKED GREBE *Podiceps nigricollis.*

One or two records, including a bird collected at Beirut in December. Lebanon lies just south of the breeding range in Europe and Asia. It has bred in Cyprus. (See pages 12, 13.)

RED-NECKED GREBE *Podiceps grisegena.*

Breeds as far south as Asia Minor. One record Beirut harbour, January. Winter, neck grey, cheeks whitish, dark cap to eye. (Crested Grebe shows white eyebrow.)

GREAT CRESTED GREBE *Podiceps cristatus.*

Has bred in Palestine and Cyprus, but only one record here, estuary of Nahr el Kelb, October. (See pages 12, 13.)

Family PELECANIDAE

WHITE PELICAN *Pelecanus onocrotalus.*

Breeding places are not far away, but it is only occasionally seen off the Lebanon coast. (See pages 12, 13.)

DALMATIAN PELICAN *Pelecanus crispus.*

One record. Breeds from south-east Europe east to mid and south Asia. Enormous, whitish. In flight shows blackish secondaries and black primaries above. Whitish from beneath. (See White Pelican pages 12, 13.)

PINK-BACKED PELICAN *Pelecanus rufescens.*

Breeds in Africa. A spring record at Beirut. Smaller than above. Wings usually brown. Breeding plumage white, dark flight-feathers, ruddy flush on back and rump.

Family PHALACROCORACIDAE

CORMORANT *Phalacrocorax carbo.*

Very few records. Most likely to be seen in winter. (See page 5.)

[SHAG *Phalacrocorax aritotelis.*]

Although it breeds in Cyprus, unrecorded in Lebanon. (See page 5.)

Family ANHINGIDAE

[DARTER *Anhinga rufa.*]

Though it breeds from Lake Antioch and Lake Huleh, only just outside Lebanon, southward in the Levant to Africa, it is not yet recorded here. Like a long, slender cormorant, with long, thin bill, head and neck like heron or crane. Black with chestnut and white. Female brown and black. Young pale underneath.

Family ARDEIDAE

BITTERN *Botaurus stellaris.*

A number of records. Seems to be occasional winter visitor. Breeds in Europe, Asia and Africa. (See pages 12, 13.)

CATTLE EGRET *Bubulcus ibis.*

Occasionally recorded on passage. Worldwide breeding range. Like Little Egret but shorter neck, paler bill. Bill and legs red at breeding time.

Family THRESKIORNITHIDAE

SPOONBILL *Platalea leucorodia.*

Widely scattered breeding areas, north, east, south and west of Lebanon. Recorded only very occasionally. (See pages 12, 13.)

GLOSSY IBIS *Plegadis falcinellus*

Range as Spoonbill. Only one record. Dark bronze. Whimbrel-shape, including curved bill but larger with longer neck.

Family PHOENICOPTERIDAE

GREATER FLAMINGO *Phoenicopterus ruber.*

Only a few records. (See pages 12, 13.)

Family ANATIDAE

[GREY LAG GOOSE *Anser anser.*]

Breeds in Europe and Asia. Winters south to North Africa and south Asia. Occurs in Cyprus chiefly in hard winters. Not yet recorded in Lebanon but surely occurs. (See pages 12, 13.)

WHITE-FRONTED GOOSE *Anser albifrons.*

A northern species migrating southward. Only one record, but must occur often. (See pages 12, 13, 193).

[BEAN GOOSE *Anser fabalis.*]

A northern species migrating southward. No certain record since Tristram, but it has occurred in Cyprus in winter. Like Grey Lag Goose but darker. Black and yellow bill.

RUDDY SHELDUCK *Tadorna ferruginea.*

Breeds in countries near Lebanon, but only one record here. Very large rusty-buff duck, with pale head, chiefly white wings with black flight-feathers and tail. (See page 193.)

SHELDUCK *Tadorna tadorna.*

Breeds to the north in Europe and Asia, wintering south to Mediterranean. Very few records. (See pages 16, 193.)

[EGYPTIAN GOOSE *Alopochen aegyptiaca.*]

Though the breeding area includes Syria and Palestine and the species occurs occasionally in winter in Cyprus, it is not recorded from Lebanon, though it doubtless occurs here. Pale brownish. Darker wings, white on coverts. Back to tail black. Chestnut eye-patch and necklace.

WIGEON *Anas penelope.*

Breeds far north. Has been recorded here occasionally in autumn and winter. Large numbers seen in winter in Cyprus. (See pages 12, 13, 193.)

GARGANEY *Anas querquedula.*

Winters from Mediterranean southward, but no recent records here. Regular migrant in Jordan and in Cyprus where it has bred. (See pages 12, 13, 193.)

SHOVELER *Anas clypeata.*

Occasional winter records but regular in Cyprus. Breeds widely in the northern hemisphere. (See pages 12, 13, 193.)

[MARBLED TEAL *Anas angustirostris.*]

Though breeding in Palestine and south Turkey, not yet recorded here. Occurs in Cyprus where it formerly bred. Grey-brown, pale dapples on body, white tail, dark ear-coverts patch.

[RED-CRESTED POCHARD *Netta rufina.*]

Though wintering in Mediterranean and known on lake Antioch, unrecorded here. Differs from Pochard by orange-red head, red bill, white on flanks and wings. Female light brown, pale cheek.

POCHARD *Aythya ferina.*

Breeds in Europe and Asia and winters around the Mediterranean. Very few records here though it probably occurs often. Common winter visitor in Cyprus. (See pages 12, 13, 193.)

FERRUGINOUS DUCK or WHITE-EYED POCHARD *Aythya nyroca.*

Though breeding chiefly north and wintering north and south of Lebanon, only a few records here. (See pages 16, 193.)

[TUFTED DUCK *Aythya fuligula.*]

Though reported to have bred in Cyprus and wintering there and around Mediterranean, unrecorded here so far. Black with white flanks and underneath; white in wing. Female dark, browner.

[SCAUP *Aythya marila.*]

Northern species. Though it winters round Mediterranean, unrecorded here. Like Tufted Duck but pale grey back. Female, white patch at base of bill.

VELVET SCOTER *Melanitta fusca.*

Northern species. One record off the coast in winter. Black. White secondaries show as wing-bar when swimming, as large white patch when flapping or flying. (See page 193.)

GOLDENEYE *Bucephala clangula.*

Northern species wintering southward to Mediterranean. One winter record at sea off Beirut. Black and white; large round white spot on cheek of black head; white neck, flanks and underparts; white square in spread black wing. Female, grey, chocolate head, white collar, similar wing-pattern. (See page 193.)

Family PHASIANIDAE

[BLACK PARTRIDGE or FRANCOLIN *Francolinus francolinus.*]

Though Lebanon lies right in the area of this bird, it is still unrecorded here. (See illustration and description, page 203.)

Family GRUIDAE

CRANE *Grus grus.*

Only occasionally recorded on passage. (See pages 12, 13.)

DEMOISELLE CRANE *Anthropoides virgo.*

Very rarely recorded. Smaller than Crane, black on throat and neck extends down breast. Long white ear-covert-plumes droop down nape.

Family OTIDIDAE

GREAT BUSTARD *Otis tarda.*

Doubtfully recorded, though winter range includes Syria. Breeds further north. Enormous goose-shaped bird with longer thick legs and more ample tail. Has thick grey neck and head; tawny, black-barred back and white wings with black primaries. (See page 48.)

LITTLE BUSTARD *Otis tetrax.*

Rather doubtfully recorded. Breeds further north and winters in part of the Levant irregularly. Not half the size of above, breeding male has black and white on neck; white wings with black tips. (See page 48.)

Family RALLIDAE

PURPLE GALLINULE *Porphyrio porphyrio.*

A record for the Anti-Lebanon. Looks like giant Moorhen, but purple-blue with red legs. (See page 51.)

Family HAEMATOPODIDAE

OYSTER-CATCHER *Haematopus ostralegus.*

Rare migrant. One coastal record. Some winter in Mediterranean area. (See pages 16, 17.)

Family CHARADRIIDAE

CASPIAN PLOVER *Charadrius asiaticus.*

Rare vagrant. One spring record. It breeds in Asia and winters in Africa. (See Plate 1, page 64.)

[GOLDEN PLOVER *Pluvialis apricaria.*]

Breeds in the north and winters south to the Mediterranean. Winter visitor to Cyprus. Unrecorded in Lebanon. Probably overlooked. Above, dark, speckled yellow. Below, pale in winter, black in summer like Grey Plover. (See page 55.)

SOCIABLE PLOVER *Vanellus gregarius.*

A small flock once recorded in autumn. Breeds in Asia. Winters southward to Africa. (See Plate 1, page 64.)

[CURLEW SANDPIPER *Calidris ferruginea.*]

Not certainly recorded on Lebanon coast. Breeds in far north-east and winters southward to India and Africa. Like Dunlin, slightly longer legs and bill, white rump. Summer, rofous (no black) beneath. (See page 52.)

KNOT *Calidris canutus.*

One spring record near Beirut. Breeds in Arctic regions and winters far south. Ruff-size; plump. Winter, grey and white. Summer, rufous beneath. (See page 52.)

SANDERLING *Calidris alba.*
One spring record near Beirut. Worldwide movements as *C. canutus*, (See pages 16, 17.)

RUFF *Philomachus pugnax.*
Very occasional on passage. Breeds in northern Europe and Asia and winters southward in both. (See pages 16, 17.)

BROAD-BILLED SANDPIPER *Limicola falcinellus.*
One record at Yammouné, autumn 1964. Breeds in the Arctic and winters from the Mediterranean south and eastward. (See pages 16, 17.)

REDSHANK *Tringa totanus.*
One record. Breeds in Europe and Asia and winters southward in both and in Africa. (See pages 16, 17.)

GREENSHANK *Tringa nebularia.*
One record Beirut. Breeds in northern Europe and Asia and winters southward in both and in Africa. (See pages 16, 17.)

WHIMBREL *Numenius phaeopus.*
One or two records. Worldwide range from northern breeding areas to southern winter ones. (See pages 12, 13.)

BLACK-WINGED STILT *Himantopus himantopus.*
Occasional on passage. World range. Partly migratory. (See pages 12, 13, 52.)

AVOCET *Recurvirostra avosetta.*
Occasional on passage though only semi-migratory. Breeds in Europe and Asia, including Jordan. (See pages 12, 13, 52.)

Family LARIDAE

HEMPRICH'S GULL *Larus hemprichii.*
One record. Breeds very locally from the coasts of Arabia and Red Sea to east and north-east Africa. (See Plate 1, page 64.)

GREAT BLACK-HEADED GULL *Larus ichthyaetus.*
One record. Breeds in parts of mid to west Asia and winters southward. (See Plate 1, page 64.)

SLENDER-BILLED GULL *Larus genei.*
Very few records. Breeds very locally near some Mediterranean coasts and Black Sea south-eastward in western Asia. Erratic in winter. (See page 64.)

COMMON GULL *Larus canus.*
Occasional in winter and on passage. Breeds widely to the north and winters southward to Mediterranean and North Africa. Herring Gull colour-pattern but smaller. Legs and finer bill greenish-yellow. (See page 70.)

BLACK TERN *Chlidonias niger.*
No records since Tristram's reference to occurrences along coast, but seen on passage in Cyprus, though less numerous than *C. leucopterus*. Breeds in Europe and Asia and winters in Africa. Black and dark grey. White under tail, pale under-wing-coverts. Winter, white underparts and head, with black nape, ear-patch and patch at side of neck-base by shoulder.

WHITE-WINGED BLACK TERN *Chlidonias leucopterus.*
Recorded occasionally offshore. Breeds in east Europe and Asia. Winters southward. Black under-wing-coverts, white rump, tail and upper wing-coverts. Winter, as Black Tern but without neck-base patch. (See page 70.)

GULL-BILLED TERN *Gelochelidon nilotica.*
No recent records. Has world range. Differs from Sandwich and Lesser Crested Terns by grey, less forked tail and short, stout, black bill. (See page 70.)

SANDWICH TERN *Sterns sandvicensis.*
Very few records. Breeds very locally on coasts of Europe, Asia, North Africa and North America and winters southward. Differs from Lesser Crested Tern by long, black bill, yellow-tipped, and white forked tail. (See page 70.)

Family COLUMBIDAE

WOOD PIGEON *Columba palumbus.*
Scarcely ever recorded. Breeds to the west, north and north-east. Mostly sedentary. Large, grey. White patch side of purple-green-glossed neck, white bar crosses wing.

Family STRIGIDAE

EAGLE OWL *Bubo bubo.*
Has been recorded from time to time in Lebanon. Breeds in Europe, Asia and Africa, including the Levant. (See pages 12, 13.)

LONG-EARED OWL *Asio otus.*
A few records only, two or three from the Cedars in times past. Breeds in northern hemisphere, including the Levant. (See pages 12, 13.)

SHORT-EARED OWL *Asio flammeus.*
Recorded occasionally from various parts of Lebanon. Presumably winter visitor. Worldwide breeding-range in the north. Winters to Mediterranean south and eastward. (See pages 12, 13.)

Family ALAUDIDAE

TEMMINCK'S HORNED LARK *Eremophila bilopha.*
A very few records in autumn. Breeds in Jordan, Syrian and Arabian deserts southward to Africa. Looks like other Horned Larks but smaller and sandy above.

Family MOTACILLIDAE

RICHARD'S PIPIT *Anthus novaeseelandiae.*
One record. Vagrant from the east or south. Large pipit, heavily streaked, longish legs and tail.

Family CORVIDAE

ROOK *Corvus frugilegus.*
No recent records. Breeds in Europe and Asia. Crow-size, black, white skin base of bill.

MAGPIE *Pica pica.*
Several were reported in southern Lebanon in October 1967, and others in August 1968 by four or five observers. The Eurasian breeding range includes Cyprus and parts of the Levant, and unless this conspicuous, long-tailed, green-glossed, black-and-white bird was overlooked hitherto, it must, surely, have wandered into the area after the breeding season, or spread its range to Lebanon recently. (See page 119.)

Family MUSCICAPIDAE

RIVER WARBLER *Locustella fluviatilis.*

Rare on passage. Breeds to the north in Europe and Asia. Winters in Africa. Plain brown above, white beneath with faint streaks on breast.

GRASSHOPPER WARBLER *Locustella naevia.*

As *fluviatilis*. Brown above, strongly streaked. Buff-white beneath, slightly streaked. Creeps in thick undergrowth.

GOLDCREST *Regulus regulus.*

Seen occasionally, usually in autumn and winter. Breeds in Europe and Asia to Turkey and Syria. Goldcrest and Firecrest, the smallest birds to visit Lebanon. Colour, olive-green with yellow and black crested stripe on crown and double wing-bars. Firecrest greener above, orange wash on shoulder, black-and-white stripes through eye and cheek and brighter orange crest-stripe. (See page 81.)

FIRECREST *Regulus ignicapillus.*

Very few records. Probably winter vagrants from Europe. (See Goldcrest.)

RED-BREASTED FLYCATCHER *Ficedula parva.*

Breeds in parts of Europe and Asia. Very few records. Probably vagrants on passage to India. Small-Warbler-size; male as shown, female and immature without orange-red, but recognized by white panels in tail. (See page 81.)

RED-FLANKED BLUETAIL *Tarsiger cyanurus.*

Only one record, October. Vagrant from north Asia. Blue above, whitish below, orange flanks. Female brown, blue rump and tail.

Family SITTIDAE

NUTHATCH *Sitta europaea.*

No recent records. Like Rock Nuthatch but warmer buff below, bluer above, spots of white on tail-tip. Creeps in trees.

DUCKS AND GOOSE IN FLIGHT (OPPOSITE)

(See pages 12–16, 187–188 and 202.)

1. Mallard, male and female
2. Teal, male and female
3. Pintail, male and female
4. Wigeon, male and female
5. Garganey, male and female
6. Shoveler, male and female
7. Pochard, male and female
8. Ferruginous Duck, beneath and above
9. Goldeneye, male and female
10. Ruddy Shelduck
11. Shelduck
12. Velvet Scoter
13. White-fronted Goose
14. Gadwall

1.
2.
3.
4.
5.
6.
7.
8.
9.
10.
11.
12.
13.
14.

APPENDIX I

HINTS ON THE RECOGNITION OF SAILING EAGLES

These notes and diagram-drawings are taken from several loaned to me by Peter Hayman who has helped many bird-watchers trying to identify raptors on passage.

SPOTTED EAGLE

Mr Hayman remarks: This is a slow, heavy, stocky bird with heavy, flapping flight—plods along as against airy flight of Lesser Spotted. Shows seven primary-tips and thus heavy-ended wings. Short, slightly wedge-shaped tail. May be well spotted with plainer body and orange-brown patch on lower abdomen. Usually (especially juveniles) very dark compared with Lesser Spotted. Head medium.

LESSER SPOTTED EAGLE

Head sticks fairly far forward, shows six primary-tips on wing, easy flight, longish wedge tail.

STEPPE EAGLE

(Eastern race, *A.r. nipalensis*): Huge bird, small head, short tail (appears to have none when approaching), large wings, drooping when sailing, showing seven primary tips. (Russian) Steppe Eagle, *A.r. orientalis*: Square wings, broader than Lesser Spotted Eagle, long carpel length, shows seven primary-tips, small head well forward, shortish tail. Has juvenile plumage spotted like Lesser Spotted, but with orange, not white, though showing white on upper tail coverts.

WHITE-TAILED EAGLE

Grinds along, flap, flap, flap, flap, never stops—rounded, vast wing-ends, yellow feet like door-knockers, prominent head, wedge-shaped tail.

IMPERIAL EAGLE

Very square-tipped tail when closed, slightly V-shaped when spread open. Shows seven primary-tips.

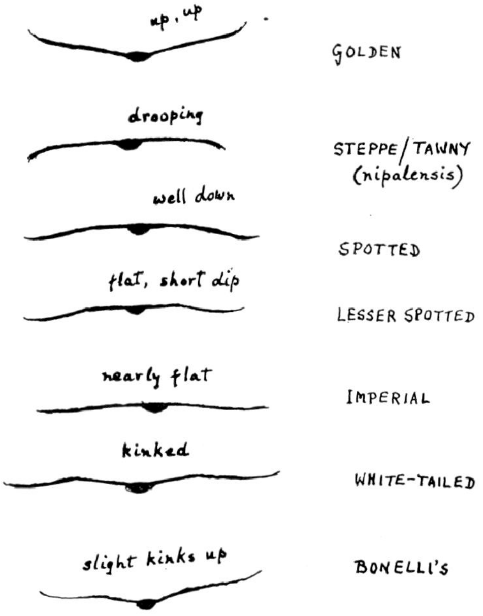

TAWNY EAGLE
FROM BENEATH

FROM PHOTO BY JOHN RAINES

NOTE PRIMARIES MISSING IN RIGHT WING. ORANGE-TAWNY TINT WHERE LIGHT CATCHES BREAST.

LESSER SPOTTED EAGLE
IMMATURE from beneath soaring with spread tail.
After P.J. HAYMAN.

SPOTTED EAGLE
IMMATURE from beneath sailing with closed tail.
After P.J. HAYMAN.

APPENDIX I

Dr John Raines, writing of eagles in East Africa, says that he sees little difference between the flight silhouettes of Steppe and Tawny Eagles and the Spotted Eagle, *A. clanga*, though he has taken a great many photographs of them.

He also mentions that he finds some attitudes of *A. pomarina*, Lesser Spotted Eagle, in flight are indistinguishable from *A. clanga*, unless the longer tail of the former is visible. The tail, however, when spread may look just like that of *A. clanga*.

1. STEPPE EAGLE. Dark type.

2. STEPPE EAGLE. Brown type.

3. SPOTTED EAGLE.

4 to 7. LESSER SPOTTED EAGLES.

8. LESSER SPOTTED EAGLE. Immature from above. (After P. Hayman.)

9. IMPERIAL EAGLE. Immature.

10. BONELLI'S EAGLE. Typical.

11. BONELLI'S EAGLE. Brown type.

12. BOOTED EAGLE.

With the exception of number 8, all the drawings opposite of flying eagles are taken from photographs made by Dr John Raines from beneath.

The size of each is not in true proportion to the rest, as some are further from the camera than others. Note the wide, square wings of Steppe Eagles, the squared tail of Imperial, the blackish under wing-coverts of Bonelli's, and the reverse wing-pattern of Booted Eagle.

Looking up at Eagles. (See captions opposite.)

APPENDIX I

Philip Stead writes from experiences, chiefly in Spain and Greece.

BONELLI'S EAGLE

'The underside of the wings are nearly black and contrast strongly with the white body. In relation to its size this bird has longer wings and a longer tail than any other European eagle and resembles a large falcon. The adults nearly always show a white spot in the centre of the back when sailing round. The immature, brown all over, is rather undistinguished except for silhouette.

BOOTED EAGLE

Has an unbanded tail, and the pale phase always reminds me of Egyptian Vulture from underneath. Most of the pale birds, especially in Spain, show a dark line through the eye like an Osprey and have a pale line from the carpal joint to the trailing edge of the wing with a pale rump. These markings look nearly white in strong sunlight.' In *Birds of Prey of the World* (Grossman and Hamlet) this is described as buff upper wing-coverts and buff crossing lower back. Philip Stead continues, 'I have seen a Booted Eagle sailing round with a Common Buzzard in Spain, and the Buzzard is actually larger. The dark phase is not at all easy to distinguish from some Common or Honey Buzzards, although the unbanded tail and heavier head are good guides.

LONG-LEGGED BUZZARD

Adult has rufous underwing coverts, which look quite foxy as the bird turns in strong sunlight, and contrast with pale primaries and secondaries. The tail is also a pale foxy brown. Perched it can look like a Rough-legged Buzzard, particularly if it is an old bird with rather washed-out plumage.

LEVANT SPARROW HAWK

Has dark eyes, not yellow ones, and a prominent yellow cere. This gives it a much kinder expression than the ordinary Sparrow Hawk. The back is a rather beautiful dove grey colour in all the individuals I have seen, and male and female are about the same size. The immature is brown—fairly dark on the back. In the adult the dove grey extends on to the head and cheeks. The dark wing-tips are also a good guide. In display flight it looks like a miniature Montagu's Harrier.

Drawings by Philip J. Stead (opposite)

1 and 2. Bonelli's Eagle.

3 and 4. Booted Eagle.

5. Short-toed Eagle.

6. Long-legged Buzzard.

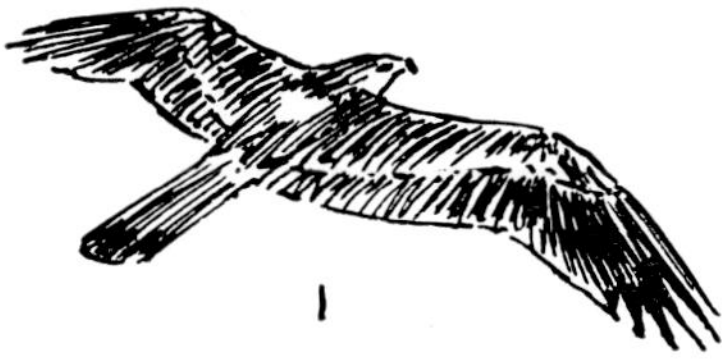

1

2

3

4

5

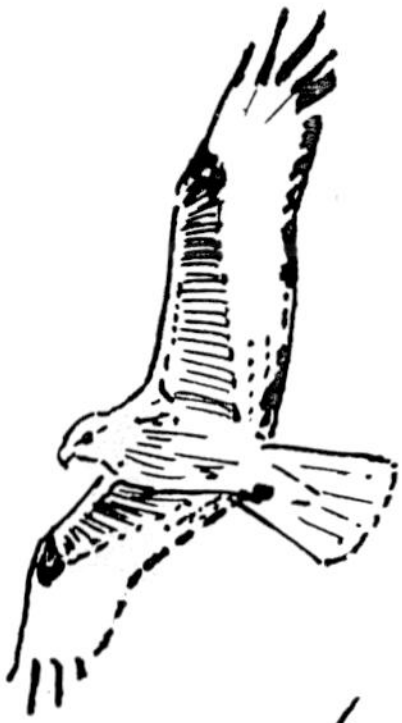

6

PIED WHEATEAR *Oenanthe pleschanka*

When in autumn or winter plumage, this is the blackest-looking of the pied-type wheatears. The Mourning Wheatear, in common with the Finsch's, Black-eared and Desert Wheatears (which travel shorter distances on migration, or are resident in their breeding areas) shows little change in autumn-winter plumage. But many individuals of the Pied become nearly all black above, except for whitish superciliary stripe, as illustrated here, with brownish-black (sometimes nearing slaty-black) on the hood and wing-coverts, dappled by narrow pale edgings, as well as black upper back, wings, face and throat (more slightly dappled) and having an orange or orange-pink flush on the upper breast. The white rump and the tail-pattern are unchanged.

WHITE-THROATED OR PERSIAN ROBIN *Irania gutturalis*

The male plumage is extremely variable in colour and pattern on the underparts. Fig. 1 shows the most common phase, with orange-chestnut breast, white throat and black cheeks, ear-coverts and sides of neck. Fig. 2 shows a narrow black band dividing the white throat from the tawny breast, and said by Meinertzhagen to be a phase of immature male. Fig. 3 shows another male variation, with the black on the neck increased and reaching to the upper breast, with only a narrow white band down the centre of the throat. Fig. 4 shows an uncommon variation with a creamy-white breast below the white throat. In most other specimens the breast varies from light, yellowish-buff to deep orange-chestnut, flame, or brick-red.

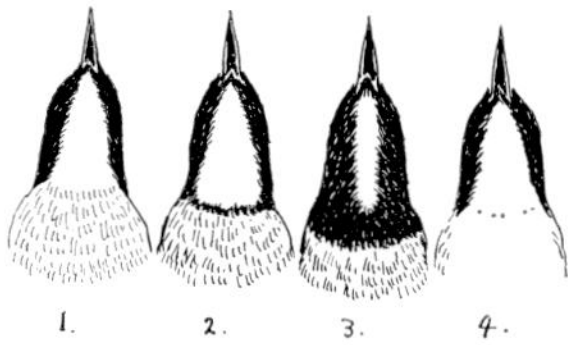

Plumage Variations of Persian Robin—The Throat-pattern

1. Normal male.
2. Said to be immature male.
3. Variation. See description from Iraq.
4. Less common creamy-white-breasted variation.

'A skulker in thick bush in its winter quarters and on passage, rather preferring ravines and hill slopes. . . . Food is entirely insects taken on the ground, birds turning over leaves when searching' (Meinertzhagen).

'It has a fine, loud song. It is clear and bubbling, somewhat recalling the European Robin. Both the male and the female seem to sing, both when in flight and when perched' (L. Cornwallis).

'Chin black, or with two black gular stripes and a central white stripe. Throat and ear-coverts black, breast a bright rufous brick (in another, chest and belly washed pink), belly, under tail-coverts white; . . . black under tail is conspicuous when lifted. It cocks tail up and spreads it, . . . flits from bush to bush like a warbler. Aggressive behaviour, singing at an intruder. The song when not in flight consists of short stretches of rich bursts with grating passages. In flight a full, rich, loud song, fluttering with wings drooped and tail fanned, is most striking. Habitat, fairly dense scrub on rocky hillside. It is not an easy bird to watch' (Moor & Boswell, from Iraq).

APPENDIX II

SOME BIRDS OF JORDAN (*not on the Lebanon List*)

For the benefit of bird-watchers in Jordan and other neighbouring countries who may be using this book, the following additional list is given. This is not a full list of Jordan's birds, but it contains some additional species which have been recorded there recently but which are not yet on the Lebanon list. Most of Jordan's breeding birds are already dealt with in this book under the heading of each species; see, for example, the following Larks: Dunn's, Desert, Bifasciated, Temminck's Horned and Lesser Short-toed; also Spur-winged, Kentish and Greater Sand Plovers, and many other species which breed in Jordan. The birds of Syria and some other neighbouring countries are, for the most part, identical with those of Lebanon and Jordan. In defining Jordan, the pre-1968 borders are envisaged.

This additional list has been picked out from the fuller one which is given in *Portrait of a Desert* by Guy Mountfort, from a list from Azraq sent to me by I. J. Ferguson-Lees, and from my own records.

V. = Vagrant; P.M. = Passage migrant; B. = Breeds; S.V. = Spring visitor.

V. YELLOW-BILLED EGRET *Egretta intermedia*
Size between Great and Little Egrets. (See pages 8, 9.)

P.M.* GADWALL *Anas strepera*
Male, darkish-grey with brown head, whitish belly, black rear. Female brown. Both have some chestnut and black in wings with a square of white on rear edge showing in flight. A little smaller than Mallard. (See p. 193.)

B.* BEARDED VULTURE *Gypaetus barbatus*
Very large bird. Grey-black upperparts, wings and tail, bright orange-buff underparts, whitish face with black patch round eye to bill and beard. Long, slender wings and long, narrow wedge-tail make it unique in flight.

V. LAPPET-FACED VULTURE *Torgos tracheliotus*
Huge, dark brown; distinguished from Cinereous Vulture by bright pink or red skinny head and throat and whitish thighs of adult seen from beneath. (See page 35.)

B?* BARBARY FALCON *Falco pelegrinoides*
Smaller and paler than Peregrine, with orange patch on nape. (See pages 40, 41.)

B. SAND PARTRIDGE *Ammoperdix heyi*

Small, sandy. Male, vinaceous grey head, white ear-coverts patch, long dark stripes along flanks. Female barred all over with light brown. Smaller than Chukar. (See page 46.)

B? BLACK PARTRIDGE or FRANCOLIN *Francolinus francolinus*

Almost as large as Chukar. (See page 46.) Male, black beneath and on the throat, boldly spotted with white on black flanks and upper mantle, and with a white patch on the cheek. It has a broad, bright chestnut collar round the neck. Lower back, rump and tail are barred black and white. Wings tawny, patterned with dark brown, abdomen and under the tail rufous. Female, same pattern in buff, brown and chestnut, with pale head and underparts.

B? WHITE TAILED PLOVER *Vanellus leucurus*

Size of Spur-winged Plover. (See page 57.) Vinaceous brown with grey on breast, vinaceous belly, white tail, black and white wings and long yellow legs.

P.M.* TURNSTONE *Arenaria interpres*

Size of Greater Sand Plover. (See page 64.) Sturdy, with orange legs. Summer, black, white and chestnut on breast, neck, head, and back; winter dark brown above, dark kidney-shaped bib. In flight, shows wide black and white bands on tail and wings.

P.M.* SPOTTED REDSHANK *Tringa erythropus*

Rather larger than Redshank. Very dark to blackish in summer, grey and white in winter, with longer bill and without white band on rear edge of wing. (See pages 16, 17.)

P.M.* MARSH SANDPIPER *Tringa stagnatilis*

Like tiny, slender, long-legged Greenshank with thin, straight bill. (See pages 16, 17.)

P.M.* BLACK-TAILED GODWIT *Limosa limosa*

P.M.* BAR-TAILED GODWIT *Limosa lapponica*

Both Whimbrel-size. Black-tailed has wide blackish and white bands along wings, black tail and white tail-coverts. Bar-tailed has narrow dark bars on tail and white rump. Both, long straightish bills (not down-curved); Bar-tailed's slightly up-curved. Summer, both rufous on head, neck and breast, and Bar-tailed on all underparts. Winter, both whitish beneath, darkish above, Black-tailed the darker. (See page 13.)

P.M.* CURLEW *Numenius arquata*
Like Whimbrel but larger, with longer down-curved bill and without crown-stripes. Clear, musical calls. (See pages 12, 13.)

V.* SLENDER-BILLED CURLEW *Numenius tenuirostris*
Whimbrel-sized Curlew but with slightly longer bill and blackish spots on sides of whitish breast and flanks. (See page 13.)

P.M. RED-NECKED PHALAROPE *Phalaropus lobatus*
Small wader (Dunlin-size) with small, thin bill, often seen swimming. Dark grey and white, rufous neck in summer. Shows long white wing-bar in flight. (See page 52.)

V. S.V. WHITE-EYED GULL *Larus leucopthalmus*
(See Plate 1, page 64.) Seen often at Aqaba in spring, usually in immature plumage. A little larger than Mediterranean and Black-headed Gulls. Rather like Hemprich's Gull, specially when immature, but is slighter, more slender, a little smaller and has, in adult plumage, a black head and throat (not dark brown), with a whitish eye and white eye-ring. The upperparts are of a greyer brown than with Hemprich's, and the bill red, black-tipped, the legs dull yellow. Immature differs from immature Hemprich's in being smaller, more slender, having dull reddish bill instead of 'slate-blue with black and red tip' (Pread & Grant).

P.M.* WHISKERED TERN *Chlidonias hybrida*
Distinguished from Black Tern and White-winged Black Tern in summer by dark grey (not black) underparts, and white cheeks and neck contrasting with black cap. (See pages 70, 190.)

B.* PIN-TAILED SANDGROUSE *Pterocles alchata*
Like a small partridge with short 'furry' legs and long, very thin points to central tail-feathers. Light grey, yellow-patterned plumage with black borders to breast-bands and white underparts. Summer male has black throat, rusty breast band and some wine-red on forewing.

B.* SPOTTED SANDGROUSE *Pterocles senegallus*
Distinguished from Pin-tailed by rather uniform pale buff underparts without yellow, rust or black breast-bands, but with black patch on abdomen. Male has yellow throat, female is finely spotted all over above and across upper breast.

V. LONG-TAILED DOVE *Oena capensis*
Very tiny pale grey and brownish dove with long, pointed, dark tail, and darkish bars on rump. Male has black face and throat.

B.* STRIATED SCOPS OWL *Otus brucei*
Paler than *O. scops*, usually greyer. (See pages 65, 77.)

B? NUBIAN NIGHTJAR *Caprimulgus nubicus*
Smaller than Nightjar. Greyish, streaked and vermiculated; russet collar and base of primaries. (See page 80.)

B? EGYPTIAN NIGHTJAR *Caprimulgus aegyptius*
Pale and sandy with some inconspicuous fine dark barring and streaks. (See page 80.)

B. PALE CRAG MARTIN *Hirundo obsoleta*
Like Crag Martin but a little smaller, paler, slightly greyer. (See page 92.)

B. BAR-TAILED DESERT LARK *Ammomanes cincturus*
Like Dunn's Lark but with finer bill, unstreaked crown, throat and mantle, and different tail. This is pinkish-buff, as the rest of the plumage, with a blackish band at the end (not black with orange-buff central feathers, as with Dunn's). (See pages 65, 94.)

B.* THICK-BILLED LARK *Rhamphocorys clot-bey*
Large, stout, sandy lark with massive bill, spotted breast, blackish and white bars in wing and black and white patches on cheeks and sides of neck.

V. CITRINE WAGTAIL *Motacilla citreola*
Summer male, head, neck and underparts clear, bright yellow, upperparts more like White Wagtail, being grey and black with white feather-edges. Female paler and tinted with brown, and winter male has only faded yellow with some grey on crown. (See pages 107–109.)

B. TRISTRAM'S GRACKLE *Onychognathus tristramii*
Rather like a Spotless Starling with bright orange patch in primaries conspicuous in flight, and rather longer tail.

B. BROWN-NECKED RAVEN *Corvus ruficollis*
As Raven, but slighter build and less heavy bill and head make it look like a black crow, with dark red-brown neck difficult to detect in the field. (See page 119.)

B.* FAN-TAILED RAVEN *Corvus rhidipurus*
Wide wings and extremely short, wide tail at once distinguish it from other Ravens and Crows. (See page 119.)

V. AQUATIC WARBLER *Acrocephalus paludicola*
Like Sedge Warbler with central pale stripe on dark-striped crown. (See pages 123, 125.)

B.* CLAMOROUS REED WARBLER *Acrocephalus stentcreus*
Rather smaller than Great Reed Warbler, but very like it. (See pages 123 and 126.)

V.* DESERT WARBLER *Sylvia nana*
Very pale sandy to greyish-sandy above and whitish below. Very small.

B. STREAKED SCRUB WARBLER *Scotocerca inquieta*
Rather like Graceful Warbler but with bigger, squarer streaked head, unstreaked back, and less conspicuously graduated and lengthy tail, the latter without the black spots on the ends of the tail-feathers. Very restless, with excited, jerky movements. (See page 161.)

B? EASTERN PIED WHEATEAR *Oenanthe picata*
Black-bellied form called Strickland's Wheatear *O.p.opistholeuca*.

B.* TRISTRAM'S or RED-RUMPED WHEATEAR *Oenanthe moesta*
A large Wheatear. Male, black face and throat to sides of neck and mantle. Crown, nape and underparts white or whitish. Rump creamy-white, slightly washed orange-buff on tail-coverts. Tail brownish-black with rusty-red base visible on outer feathers. Wings less black than mantle, washed brownish-grey with secondaries and coverts pale-edged or white-edged. Female, pale sandy-brown above and creamy-white beneath with rusty-buff head and nape to upper mantle, and dark brown tail showing more rusty-red at the base, and creamy rump.

V. RED-TAILED WHEATEAR *Oenanthe xanthoprymna*
Grey-brown above, whitish eyebrow-stripe, black face and throat, whitish beneath, orange-rusty rump, tail-pattern as with Wheatear, of black and white or black and rust. (See page 145.) One phase has the ear-coverts dark red-brown and the throat nearly white with a rusty wash on underparts and brown and rust in tail. Females are similar to the last phase.

B? HOODED WHEATEAR *Oenanthe monacha*
A large Wheatear with a rather long bill. Spring male has white crown and nape to upper mantle, white underparts and rump and almost entirely white tail-feathers with brown central pair

and a brown mark on outer pair. The centre-back, face, throat, upper breast and sides of neck to back are black. Female is very pale brown above, pale buff beneath and buff on the rump and outer tail-feathers, brown on central tail-feathers.

B. WHITE-CROWNED BLACK WHEATEAR *Oenanthe leucopyga*
Adult, both sexes, black all over except for white crown, rump, outer tail-feathers and from vent to under tail. Immature and young adult birds have no white 'skull-cap'.

B. BLACKSTART *Cercomela melanura*
Pale grey-brown with black rump and tail. About Redstart-size.

B. ARABIAN BABBLER *Turdoides squamiceps*
About the size of a thrush, but with a long, graduated tail; pale, silvery brown, paler beneath, with scaly appearance on crown to mantle. Seen in parties or small flocks in bushes.

B. DEAD SEA SPARROW *Passer moabiticus*
A small Sparrow, handsomely marked with black on chestnut back and wings. Grey cheek divided from black bib by white moustache-stripe and bright yellow patch at sides of throat and neck. Female has less yellow and no black bib.

B. SINAI ROSEFINCH *Carpodacus synoicus*
About Greenfinch-size. Male has forehead, face, throat, underparts and rump deep, vivid crimson-rose-pink. Nape and back pinkish-brown, wings and tail brown. Female brownish.

B. HOUSE BUNTING *Emberiza striolata*
Very small Bunting. Male tawny with streaked mantle, bright tawny-rust wing-coverts and edges of flight-feathers, dark tail with tawny outer edges, pale tawny underparts. Head streaked white and black with white eyebrow-stripe. Chin and throat to upper breast grey-black with white borders to feathers. Female less brightly tinted, with dark streaks on buff head.

Most of the first eleven species marked* are migrants which are just as likely to be recorded in Lebanon as elsewhere in the Near East, with the exception of the Bearded Vulture and the Barbary Falcon, which, like the remaining eight so marked (excluding Clamorous Warbler) are birds of the desert or semi-desert, including Syrian desert, and thus not unlikely to be recorded in Lebanon at any time.

The Clamorous Reed Warbler inhabits reed-beds and has bred regularly at Huleh, almost on the Lebanon border.

Nearly all the remaining species in this list are found no further north or west than the Dead Sea area. Most of these breed in southwest Asia and in Africa.

*Not unlikely to occur within or near Lebanon's borders.

REFERENCES

Ali, Sálim, 1941: *The Book of Indian Birds* (Bombay Natural History Society).
Ali, Sálim, 1949: *Indian Hill Birds* (Oxford University Press).
Bannerman, D. A. and W. M., 1958: *Birds of Cyprus* (Oliver & Boyd, Edinburgh).
Brown, L. & Amadon, D., 1968: *Eagles, Hawks and Falcons of the World.* (For Country Life Books, by Hamlyn Publishing Group, Feltham, Middlesex.)
Christensen, S., Nielsen, B. P., Christensen, N. H. and Sorensen, L. H. 1968: Field Identification of Aquila-Eagles. *Dansk Ornithologisk Forenings* Tidsskrift 62, 1968. 1. (Copenhagen).
Goodwin, D., 1949: Notes on the Migration of Birds of Prey over Suez. *Ibis*, Vol. 91, No. 1.*
Grossman, M., & Hamlet, J., 1965: *Birds of Prey of the World* (Cassells, London).
Hollom, P. A. D., 1959: Notes from Jordan, Lebanon, Syria, Antioch. *Ibis*, Vol. 101, No. 2.*
Jones, M., 1965: Bimaculated Lark. *British Birds*, Vol. 58, No. 8.†
Kumerloeve, H., 1962: *Notes on the Birds of the Lebanese Republic.*‡
Mackintosh, D. R., 1949: Use of Thermal currents by Birds on Migration. *Ibis*, Vol. 91, No. 1.*
Mackworth-Praed, C. W., & Grant, C. H. B., 1952: *Birds of Eastern and North Eastern Africa* (Longmans, Green & Co., London, New York, Toronto).
Marchant, S., 1963: Notes on Iraqi Birds (discussion S. melanocephala/S. mystacea). *Bulletin, B.O.C.*, Vol. 83, pages 53–54.*
Meinertzhagen, R., 1954: *Birds of Arabia* (Oliver & Boyd).
Meinertzhagen, R., 1930: *Nicoll's Birds of Egypt* (Hugh Rees, Ltd, London).
Meinertzhagen, R., 1954: Some Aspects of Spring Migration in Palestine. *Ibis*, Vol. 96, No. 2.*
Moor & Boswell, 1956: *Field Observations on Birds of Iraq*, Parts 1, 2 and 3.§
Mountfort, G., 1965: *Portrait of a Desert* (Collins, London).
Nielsen, Bent Pors and Christensen, Steen, 1969: On the Autumn Migration of Spotted Eagles and Buzzards in the Middle East. *Ibis*, Vol. III, No. 4.*
Peterson, R. T., Mountfort, G., Hollom, P. A. D., 1954: *Field Guide to Birds of Britain and Europe* (Collins, London).
Pyman, G. A., 1953: Autumn Raptor Migration in Eastern Mediterranean. *Ibis*, Vol. 95, No. 3.*
Simmons, K. E. L., 1954: Behaviour and General Biology of Graceful Warbler, 'Prinia gracilis'. *Ibis*, Vol. 96, No. 2.*
Stead, P. J., 1965: European Bustards. *British Birds*, Vol. 58, No. 2.†
Vaurie, C., 1959, 1965: *The Birds of the Palearctic Fauna* (Witherby, London).
Wallace, D. I. M., 1964: Hippolais Warblers. *British Birds*, Vol. 57, No. 7.†
Williamson, K., 1962, 1963, 1964: *B.T.O. Identification Guides.* (Brit. Trust for Ornithology, Tring, England.)
Witherby, W. F., Jourdain, F. C. R., Ticehurst, N. F., Tucker, B. W., 1938: *The Handbook of British Birds.* (Witherby, London.)

* (British Ornithologists' Union, British Museum (Natural History), London.)
† (Witherby, London.) ‡ (Iraq Nat. Hist. Museum Publication, Nos. 20, 21.)
§ (Iraq Nat. Hist. Museum Publication. Iraq Natural History Institute, Waziriya No. 5/3/9, Baghdad, Iraq.)

INDEX

INDEX